Living Happily
By Your Own Design

Pathways to Personal Power

Dr. Pamela Ladd

2nd Tier Publishing

Published by:
2nd Tier Publishing
501 Wimberley Oaks Dr
Wimberley, TX 78676-4671, U.S.A.

ISBN 978-0-578-07564-8

Cover photograph by Norm Ladd
Book and cover design by Dan Gauthier

Acknowledgements

Much of what I have learned about life and being happy has come from my parents Harold and Etta McCullough, I thank them for loving me, believing in me, and being great examples. For reading every word, finding mistakes, and making this a much better book, I thank Lois Arlene Miller. For challenging me, asking me for clarity, and sometimes gently prodding, I sincerely thank Kim Torgerson for the hard work of being my editor. For loving me and believing in me, I am grateful to my children Simon and Joy, and all my family and friends. To my husband Norm who lovingly supports me, and loved my book enough to portray his art, The Fourth Monkey, on the cover, I give my unending gratitude and love.

Contents

Contents

About the Author

Pamela Ladd works as a Life Coach, has been an entrepreneur for over two decades, and is an entertaining speaker. She challenges her personal boundaries daily and lives her life with humor and passion. Pamela is a fearless adventurer of life, and she has explored the world on foot. In her private practice, Pamela is an intuitive listener, a gifted dreamworker, and a fountain of brilliant ideas. Pamela speaks on love, happiness, and human potential. She is mother of two and a grandmother of four, and lives in Bloomington, Indiana with her husband Norm and her dog Sam.

Dr. Pamela Ladd
www.PamelaLadd.com

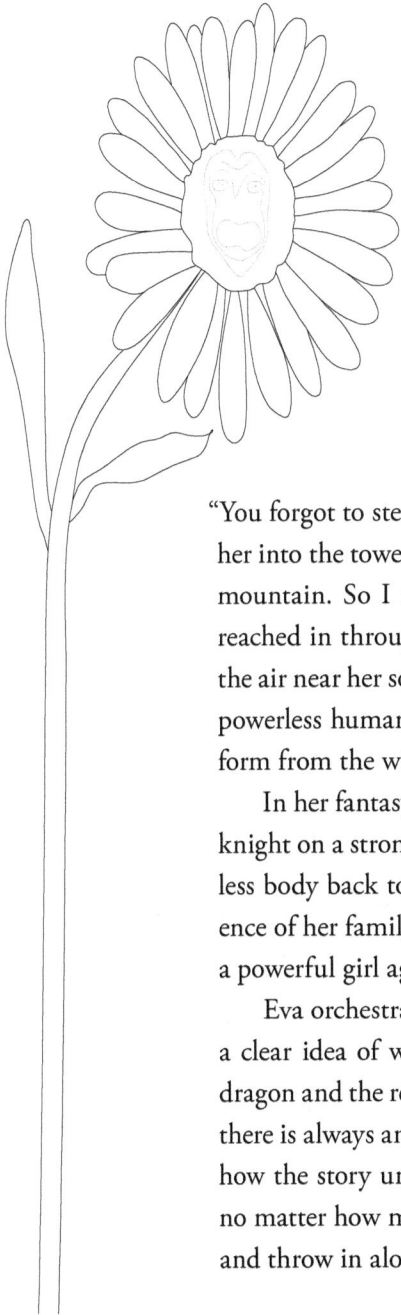

Preface

"You forgot to steal my power," Eva called out after I tossed her into the tower of a pretend castle, high atop the pretend mountain. So I turned the invisible key backwards, then reached in through the make believe door, and grabbed at the air near her solar plexus. She slumped into a limp pile of powerless human mass, waiting for me to magically transform from the witch to the knight and rescue her.

In her fantasy story three-year-old Eva is rescued by the knight on a strong horse; however, he must carry her powerless body back to her family, because it is only in the presence of her family that she regains her energy and becomes a powerful girl again.

Eva orchestrates this story from beginning to end with a clear idea of what she wants. Sometimes the witch is a dragon and the rescuer is a prince or the Tin Man. However, there is always an exchange of power. She has a clear idea of how the story unfolds and a vision of its positive outcome no matter how many twists, turns, and surprises I imagine and throw in along the course of the play.

Even at three years old, Eva has grasped the idea that power is an integral part of the game we call life. In her story the witch's power is used to dominate and suppress the power of another person. Yet Eva's fantasy is intricate and involved enough that she also experiences an exchange of power through the kindness and generosity of her family and the knight who rescues her.

Power does not have to be about dominating another person. This is very often what we think of when we use the word power, because we have seen the misuse of power in our own lives, and we see power misused every day on the television news.

Your level of happiness and authentic power will determine your ability to make manifest your desires in life. Since this is so, power is also the ability to be, to do, and to cause an action in your life. Being powerful gives you the ability to tap into the innate goodness that exists in everyone. It gives you the strength to go after what you truly want in your life. Being powerful connects you with optimism, and it is optimism that makes life worth living. When you are optimistic, purposeful, and know what you want, you realize you have the power to be happier in a world that doesn't necessarily reward happiness.

Being focused and personally powerful are the underpinnings of a richer and happier life. Each of us innately knows this. This knowledge must exist within the cellular memory of our species if a three-year-old child has a grasp of it. Do we really need the research of neuroscientists to tell us that some interpersonal relationships are harmful, and happy relationships are healthful for our heart rhythms and brain activity? Each of us feels this intuitively.

Yet I appreciate this scientific investigation because it justifies our pursuit of happiness, contentment, and satisfaction. Scientific research shows positive feelings are congruent with healthy standard body measurements, like blood pressure and heart rate. True beauty is also seen in the clear eyes and the translucent skin of the joyful person.

When you were a young child, you too probably knew exactly what you wanted out of life. But as you grew older part of your learning process was to conform and fit-in, you molded your plans and ideas to suit people and institutions outside of yourself, such as schools, your family, judgmental friends, and business associates. If somewhere along the way the life you envisioned did not manifest, or slipped further and further into the background, it is possible to grab hold of your vision and pull it forward; however, this will not happen on its own.

It is up to you to create a life you love, to figure out what excites you and how you intend to build a deep, passionate, and abundant happiness. You will find that it is working through your strengths, not working on your weaknesses that will bring you success and fulfillment. Your discovery will be profound. It will be the kind of complete rich fulfillment that spills over into the world and gives to others. To accomplish this, it is necessary to do what you truly love, and then you will get what you truly want.

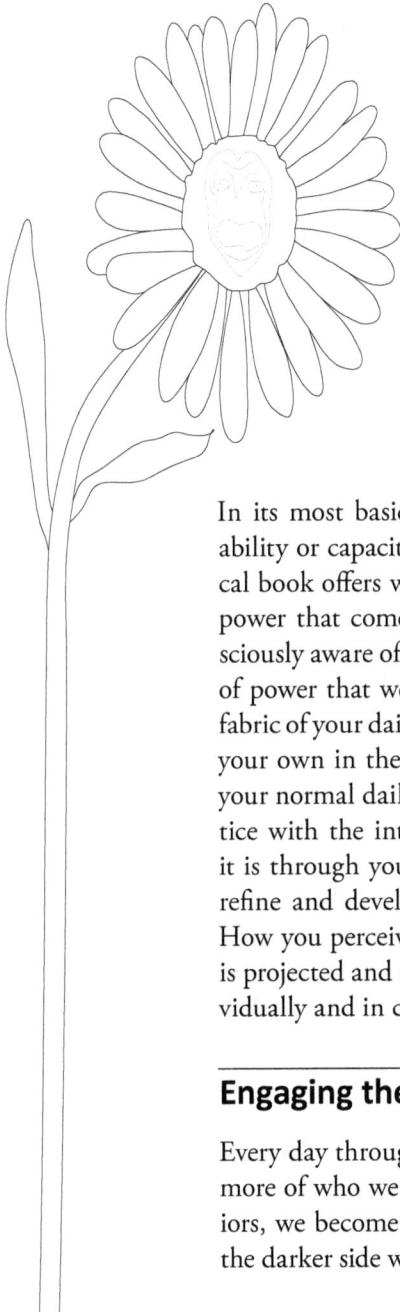

1

Enduring Power
What Is It, and What Sparks It?

In its most basic definition, the term *power* refers to the
ability or capacity to perform or act effectively. This practical book offers ways to help you build enduring power—a
power that comes from within you, shaped by being consciously aware of your desires and motivations; it is the type
of power that weaves happiness and contentment into the
fabric of your daily life, and it is power that helps you to hold
your own in the face of negativity and adversity. Through
your normal daily experiences, you will have plenty of practice with the integration of power into your life, because
it is through your interactions with other people that you
refine and develop your authenticity and personal power.
How you perceive other people and how they perceive you
is projected and recognized through all of your senses, individually and in combination.

Engaging the Power of Your Vision

Every day through our intentions and activities we become
more of who we already are. Across the spectrum of behaviors, we become more energetic, vibrant, and loving or on
the darker side we become more cruel and fearful. Through

the dynamics of our relationships and how we respond to challenges, we are either growing or withering—or maybe on some days we are simply in a holding pattern. Knowingly or unknowingly, we choose our responses and live with their consequences. A universal truth observed by Horace, a first century B.C. Roman poet, is still true today, "Power without wisdom falls of its own weight."

Being aware of how you gain and use power prepares you to employ it wisely and to be powerful in meaningful and significant ways. Being perceptive and deliberate in your actions and thinking allows you to live beyond the surface desires of your ego and reach the true power and happiness of life. Even though we are always connected with the spiritual energy of creation, sometimes that connection can feel very weak. Being aware of where we are and what we are doing helps us to realize our essential nature is to be happy and content. There is no difference between delight and divine; they are one. However, since we are alive and living here on planet Earth, our interactions take place in the physical world, and real-life specific techniques of being powerful and exuding power are needed for our own benefit and the greater good.

External displays of force—power as intimidation—are not the sustaining traits of power that support and help you when inevitable problems and trauma enter your own life. Your resilience for overcoming these situations is always built from within you.

In this book, you will also learn practical essentials to support your life—focused exercises relating to money, journaling, building relationships, caring for your health, and improving your appearance—these are always part of your power "toolbox." Claiming them and using the power they hold means actively going after what you want from your life and presenting yourself well while you do it. You cannot just go along from day to day without conscious intention and purpose and expect to be happy, successful, and attain what you want from life.

Each thought you think creates your life and creates your vision of what you think can happen for you. As you live each day, let your unique intuitive nature be part of the process. Learn to access your intuition because your thoughts and your logical mind will only take you so far when you are creating expanded possibilities and reaching into your dreams.

When you explore new options and ways to live, you will find many things you already do now, work perfectly. Accept those and congratulate yourself. Then move on to areas where your intuition is speaking to you, and its small voice is telling you to look more closely and listen more carefully to yourself. What are your dreams? What ideas keep coming back to you? What do you see?

Look at them, write them down; even if your thoughts and dreams seem paradoxical or unreasonable, do not be so quick to let your logical mind see your ideas as useless and throw them out untested. If you give up before you start, you may miss a gift; hold steady, you could be receiving a big message from a small idea.

During a very difficult time in my life, when everything seemed to be falling apart around me, I decided to re-examine everything I did. As I deconstructed my intentions and truly looked at what worked for me, I kept coming back to the concept, "walk." Not only did I find that idea very frustrating, it seemed unreasonable and simplistic. Was I deluding myself? How could walking transform my troubles? And yet, at that time in my life it did seem to be what worked best. It grounded me, was rhythmic, and was almost always possible to do. I could use walking as meditation, exercise, or as a form of transportation. Walking led me to new experiences, new friends, to many foreign lands, and it brought me to a wider more optimistic view of the world. I have even walked across Spain.

> *This is your life: live it your way and know what "living it your way" means.*
>
> *Our species has the ability to create altered realities; we constantly create realities beyond our day-to-day experience. You can easily see how we do this through music and the stories we tell; however, we can also extend our realities through our thoughts and our dreams.*

If you learn to relax, trust yourself, and become comfortable with uncertainty, you can let new ideas rain down around you, and you can float around in a sea of ambiguity and be okay with that. Paradoxes are part of your human experience, and they are part of your personal path of discovery. You will discover everything in your life holds power or the potential for it. Everything about you, your money, your time, your ideas, even the love you have, they all have potential to build joy, and all of your personal qualities, assets, capacities, and energies combine uniquely to create your personal style and precisely what is uniquely powerful for you. Living powerfully is the secret to living happily by your own design.

Each day can be another heroic adventure of your life. You can live your life well. When you are powerful you are prepared to embrace all of life, and benefit from everything the human experience has to offer: all that we consider to be good and to be bad, including the love and deception, the winning and betrayal, the sickness and health. Most importantly, you can be certain that you can handle it and even love through all of it, every bit of it.

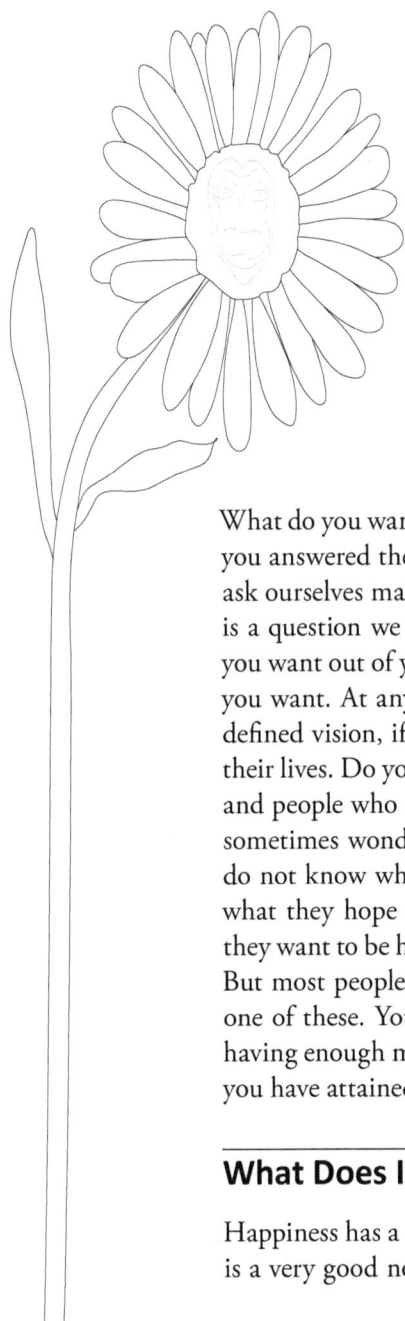

2

Getting What You Want

A Purposeful Vision for Your Life

What do you want? Have you asked yourself this lately, have you answered the query? This is a question each of us must ask ourselves many times during our life, and sometimes it is a question we must ask ourselves each day. To get what you want out of your life you must first know what it is that you want. At any given time, most people have a fuzzy ill-defined vision, if any at all, of what they want to create for their lives. Do you know what you want? Even professionals and people who have owned their own businesses for years sometimes wonder if they're in the right job. Most people do not know what it is they desire most, their purpose, or what they hope to create for their lives. I hear people say they want to be happy, be successful, or have enough money. But most people do not have a personal definition for any one of these. You must decide what happiness, success, or having enough money means to you in order to know when you have attained it.

What Does It Mean to Be Happy?

Happiness has a different meaning for each person and this is a very good notion because it makes life interesting. For you it may mean contentment, having successful relationships, or it may mean you have found a way to use your skills in service to others.

Most likely you have already discovered that happiness cannot be found in the acquisition of things. Even so, we still look at a beautiful object and think it will add to our happiness and maybe it does momentarily, but that sort of happiness is fleeting. It is necessary to purchase things for our survival, comfort, and to make life easier. Yet if we unconsciously look to objects to define who we are, our search can send us on a false trajectory. We can end up searching for happiness in the acquisition of things to the point we no longer know what we own. Buying things can get wound up in our basic fears about survival and safety that reach deep into our human history, and so it is the motivation behind the purchase that each of us must be willing to examine.

Happiness can be found in facing uncomfortable situations and facing our fears. One of those may be facing how it feels not to buy an item. The willingness to step into fearful acts, to be daring enough to examine our thoughts, and then to be uncomfortable in the process are the first steps of an exciting new journey. Are you willing to really look at yourself and discover what you are ignoring? And then when you do, will you be willing to do what it takes to make a difference? Willingness indicates a high level of consciousness; people who are successful are willing to find out what their limitations are and do what it takes to move past them. It starts with changing your mind. Here are two examples.

Dan was confident at his job working with computers at a large company, but when he was promoted, Dan would be required to give presentations and he was terrified of public speaking. He couldn't speak in front of a group without looking down and putting his hands in his pockets. When a colleague told Dan about a Toastmasters club near his job, he thought he might be laughed out of the group if he joined. However, he joined anyway and started out slowly, learned where his fears were the strongest, discovered ways to compensate for them, and was willing to try different tactics until he found a style that worked for him. Dan isn't totally over his fear of speaking publicly, but now he knows how to channel his fear and speak well anyway.

Marcia wanted to quit her corporate job and start her own company. She was afraid of leaving behind the security of a regular paycheck, health insurance, and knowing what to expect every day. But she also wanted freedom to express herself creatively. Over the years Marcia had gained a lot of skill in her job. Now she wanted to challenge her fear that she lacked the confidence and tenacity to run her own business. Marcia could have caved in, stayed with her company, and taken the easy way out; however, she was willing to accept uncertainty, to go into the unknown, to challenge her fears, and to look at what she believed about herself. She learned to value the areas in which she was an expert and to find support where she was limited. The last time we spoke, Marcia's business was profitable, growing steadily, and she was happy with her decision.

What would it take for you to find and examine your limitations, and then to overcome the presumptions you have about those boundaries, in order for you to move on to live a life of power and happiness? It takes willingness and it takes courage to examine and challenge even your simplest beliefs about yourself.

Presumptions and Assumptions

Presumptions that have gained solidity have the power to keep us locked in place. When our presumptions are solid, we will not gather any further information that could broaden our outlook and support a different position. We look the other way when a person speaks to us, and no other data has the faintest chance of getting through our filters unless it supports the idea we have already formed.

This is true for everyone; just look to how we view our politicians and how we see our friends. If you have heard yourself say about another "she always does that," then look to yourself. What assumptions have you made about who you are and what your capabilities are?

Your assumptions are embedded within you, but are they true, are they relevant? How do you know when it is time to dismantle and challenge your thoughts? If we see it as a possibility we can be more informed and conscious. Choose to be more aware, look more closely at situations that bring up emotions, thoughts, and reflexes like or similar to the following.

- ❧ When you notice that you are afraid of or resigned to something
- ❧ When you recognize a limitation and decide it is real, fixed, and unchangeable
- ❧ When you predict your behavior and find absolutely no joy in it

Dispelling fear is an important part of overcoming inertia, because the low-grade fear of trying new things and being rejected leads to anxiety and inactivity. It can be scary to truly look at yourself and evaluate your responses. What we normally do when we first start to get honest with ourselves and begin to feel vulnerable, is to jump straight back to junior high school and start to remember all of the inadequate feelings we felt back then. Worse, we add to them all the sensitivities we have gained since that time. So if you hear yourself saying, I'm fat, I'm ugly, it's too hard, and what's the point, you are not alone. Please be kind to yourself, tell that voice to be quiet and still.

A Rise in Consciousness

During the process of self-discovery and creation of new experiences, you are going to become more conscious and available to yourself and the world. With consciousness comes responsibility, you will no longer be able to engage in mean or disrespectful behavior with yourself or anyone else. As your negative inner critic rises to belittle you or react in a vengeful manner, your awareness will instantly alert you, and you will know if you are not living up to your new inner vision. Your own conscience will nag at you and make you uncomfortable when your behavior does not measure up. This knowing is a gift.

Even though it may be uncomfortable and difficult for you, it is important to let life flow at its own rate and stop trying to control it. Just notice it and feel it. There are many things out of your control. Let them be. When you stop putting your energy where it has no effect, you will have more energy left for you.

Consequently, as you become more conscious and identify what you really want for your life, your energy will be less scattered. It naturally works like this because you are not pulled in a dozen different directions as you release energy drains. When you are more focused, your work goes easier, and when you know the work is going well, you can also rest well. Being conscious puts you in the mood to recognize emotions for what they are: genuine longing, hunger, anger, loneliness, or exhaustion become friendly and familiar and you can tend to them productively. All of this occurs because you create a shift in the way you see yourself and your connection to the world.

Cultural scholar Joseph Campbell said, "When we quit thinking primarily about ourselves and our self preservation, we undergo a truly heroic transformation of consciousness." As you alter the way energy flows through you, you elevate your level of consciousness and your subjective well-being. With rising energy, you will gain the power to build what you want to build and contribute where you want to contribute. When your life is over, what lives on when you are gone are your contributions and the love you have left in your wake.

Breaking Away From Old Labels

Selfish, dumb, lazy, unavailable, what have you been called in the past? As a seventh grader, on the first day of school, I stepped up on the school bus in a brand-new dress, full of hope and excitement. A freshman boy pointed his finger at me and said, "Look at that pukey looking thing," and all of the upperclassmen laughed. For a long time after that, I carried the "pukey-looking-thing label." I carried it way too long. When I was afraid to do something, I could always pull his words out, and their memory could stop me dead-in-my-tracks. What labels or energetic burdens do you carry? What can you throw out? Do it now, don't wait.

What I want you to do is this: consciously one-by-one identify what thoughts and actions work for you as you move closer to success and happiness. Do this systematically, no pressure, just know it. What you identify as "this works" may only be slightly different from what you do now. However, you may want to make significant changes in how you use you life. Big or small, either way you will need to alter how you use your time, effort, and money to create a difference in what you get in return.

When I was insulted on the school bus, I didn't have the personal tools to protect myself from harm. I felt it would not have done any good to tell my parents, because they acted like what I thought all parents acted like; they thought I was beautiful. They were supposed to think that. As an adult I learned to say "thank you" when I received an insult. But when I started this, it was mostly just to shock the insult giver. Now with people I find difficult, I can say thank you with love and compassion and also I make the effort to see each person as being from the same creation as me. Greater awareness has helped me see that fears, hopes, and dreams can influence the behavior of any person.

Getting along with difficult people is something we all need to do, yet the basic idea behind well-being is to spend your time with people who treat you well. When you are comfortable with yourself and your personal power, you will attract people who are easy to be around and fun to be with. When I heard the Dalai Lama say, "There is no shame in walking away from people who have a harmful effect on you," I totally agreed with him.

As you become more connected with yourself and other people who bring out the best in you, you will be able to move more easily through your life. I am sure you instinctively know this to be true from your own experience. Remember the times you felt successful and how it felt in your body; you moved through life with ease, and in those times everything seemed to happen naturally for you.

Be brave as you try new activities and ask yourself new questions. Also be prepared for reactions you might not expect from those around you. You will get a lot of pressure to "stop changing" from people who love you and work with you because as you change and improve, they have to adjust to the change in you, if only by sheer physical necessity. You will receive many signals to stop what you are doing and stay the same. One reason this happens is because you do not have any history built around this new behavior. It could be your friends and family may be thinking you will not carry through, so why get invested in it. The "stop changing" messages are bound to happen because we live and thrive in social systems, which depend on familiar, continuous, and complex interconnection. Even people you see as on your side or highly evolved can react negatively when they see change occurring in you, because they feel they will lose their connection to you. This could one of the most difficult parts of your passage.

Get specific about what you want for yourself today, not what others want for you or how they have labeled you in the past. Always question yourself and challenge yourself with new questions because your truthful answers will help to bring out your authentic power. Take the time to ask yourself the questions in the box "Understanding what you want now." You will increase their impact if you answer the questions in writing or speak out loud; your own voice can clear your head or arouse your heart. Writing your responses can engage the phenomenon of inspirational writing, which connects you directly with your soul; if this happens you will go deep and

---

Understanding what you want now

Ask yourself the following questions. You will increase their impact if you respond to them in writing or speak your answers out loud; your own voice can clear your head or arouse your heart.

What brings you totally alive?

What would it take to make you happy or successful?"

Would it be doing a certain type of job?

Would you be working alone or with others?

Do you need to upgrade your skills?

Do you need to improve your relationships?

What would it take to do that?

Do you need to improve yourself?

How much money do you really need?

What are your beliefs about your ability to make money and provide for yourself?

---

learn a great deal about yourself. If your writing is intellectual, it will also give you time to think, ponder, and choose your words. Let them evolve out of your own essence and personality, and be inspired to answer the questions truthfully and completely, keeping in mind everything you already are today; and at the same time, integrate your answers with the vision of who you intend to become.

In the exercise "Understanding what you want now," what do your answers show? Do you have a vision for your life? Were you surprised at your answers, or do you clearly see what you want and how you want to live? Maybe you need to overcome inertia, climb over self-doubt, or conquer a habit of laziness. There's always the "seven deadly sins" to confront: vanity, sloth, anger, gluttony, greed, lust, and envy. Or maybe you simply need to stop the frenetic activity and relax more.

As you look through your answers, learn to assess the opinions you have formed about yourself. Why you formed them is not as important as their relevancy. To stay fresh get into the habit of rethinking how you look at the world and reassessing the decisions you make. Are you making those decisions consciously or because "that's how you've always done it?" This is your life and it is powerful to live your life consciously.

Do you see yourself repeating the same or similar mistakes you have made in the past and attracting the same problems? If you do, believe me you are not alone. Yet it does not have to be that way, you can begin today to alter how you think, by opening up and clearing out stale patterns of thought. You can live a happier life, and at the same time you can grow the business of your dreams. It is possible, if that is what you want.

Expanding Your Vision

When you have a well-developed sense of yourself, a picture of your future, and what you want, you are in a better position to recognize and take advantage of opportunities as they come along. Opportunities do happen and they will occur again, but if you are too timid or cannot recognize them, they will pass by to another person–they will not wait for you. I have seen accomplished and experienced people let magnificent opportunities fall to someone less experienced because they lacked the confidence, self-esteem, and personal vision to take advantage of them.

Missed opportunities are part of the evolution of the human experience. It is what we learn afterwards that teaches us how to live and shows us how we can change our lives for the better. Used properly an expanding vision can be a magnificent bridge to the future; however, it takes confidence, self-esteem, and personal power to clearly see where you are in life now. From here, the path opens to where you want to go.

Qualities You Admire

"We imitate only what we believe and admire," noted author Robert A Willmott. If your focus is not clear on what you are building for yourself, it is okay, slow the process, and look around you, there are plenty of outstanding people you can model. Take a piece of paper. Sit back and think about qualities and people you admire.

Then start a list. Who do you admire? What are their qualities, and how closely do you match them? If there is no one in your immediate community, look to your professional or national community. It is not even necessary for you to identify a real person. You can be creative and pick and choose traits you admire, and build a unique and original composite person. This is a life-long process; there are always competent people of high character to admire and aspirations to obtain, and from this,, you will continue to weave and to blend traits and new qualities into your personality.

Using your imagination, make this perfect person come alive:

- **First**, list the attributes and qualities of the successful person you admire.

- **Next**, across from each attribute you have chosen, jot down how closely you match that trait.

- **Last**, write a little bit about what you need to do to improve your mind-set, skills, and behavior to more closely match this person.

Keep this exercise simple. Very small changes add up to make a big difference when implemented consistently over time.

What Are Your Strengths and What Do You Value?

One way to add meaning to your life is to integrate your strengths and values. Many times we are not in touch with our strengths, and we do not spend time doing what we value. It is far better to maximize your strengths and spend your time and effort on the things you do well than to be frustrated working in areas in which you are weak, only to attain quite meager results. It take years to become skilled in any profession you choose, but you will know right away whether you find joy in it and have a talent for it.

We neglect our strengths for several reasons. Sometimes we do not value our talents and strengths because we do not see how they could make us money. Other times we see them as usual and do not recognize their uniqueness. And worst of all, we erroneously feel we are supposed to work on our weaknesses. When talented musicians or artists neglect playing an instrument or producing artwork we say, "Isn't it a shame the way they waste their talent." However it is the same for other people who have strengths and talents in various areas but do not pursue them, because they feel pressured to work at something else.

Consider the mother whose strength is a joy for homemaking and child-rearing. Yet she feels pressure from her community to be successful in the workforce doing the type of job that is currently valued, such as a corporate manager. On a deep soul level, an ill-fitted job will always mean increasingly less over time. To look within yourself, to find what is meaningful, is always difficult when you are constantly being told from an external source what is appropriate and important. It is not only women who work as homemakers who feel undervalued doing work our society deems insignificant, many people work in jobs to fulfill the dreams of other people, or they work at them for the money to reach an ever elusive social ranking. Even though it may seem impossible in the beginning, when you engage your creativity there are always ways to reinvent how you approach work.

I want you to know that if you spend time in a job where you are abused or you just go through the motions, you will never know the possibilities that could develop for you. Doing good work where you are valued makes you happy, expands you, develops your strengths, and makes you more powerful. If you are undervalued, find new options, wherever they are. You will meet people who love the things you love. If you are valued, you will see your richness, abundance, and experience grow. Wouldn't it be a shame if each one of us did not live our purpose or use and develop our strengths?

Nurturing Your Natural Creativity

It is just as important to exercise your mind and imagination as it is your body. Many of us have the false belief that we are not creative, yet we are all creative people. We have this view of ourselves because of our natural inclination to compare ourselves to others we feel are far more talented. This never works, because comparison is the gateway to suffering and discontent. Although one simply cannot fault Rembrandt, Mozart, or U2 for their genius, creativity is always very close to each of us; it is found in gardens, kitchens, and the resourcefulness of every business. It is found not only in what you make with your hands, it is also found in how you use your mind.

Creative energy brings a lot of vitality to your life. To get it going, you do not need a change in geographic location or in your relationships. Although, I do not discount the value of a good vacation, especially one that allows you to use your body in new ways, like hiking or scuba diving; or a vacation that slows you down to give you the "rest of your life."

When you are dissatisfied it is natural to think you need to change everything. Normally, that is not necessary, there is a lot working right in your life, and it is important to recognize what those things are and keep them in place. I am suggesting that within the structures you have already built, you can begin to change your perspective of the world and how you relate to it. Look for a balance between throwing everything out and holding yourself static; it is a natural state of being for you to evolve, learn, and become more powerful. Even if you want things to stay the same, nothing in your life is static.

Your natural creativity will work to help you reshape your outlook, once you decide that is what you want. Relax and give your creative imagination a chance to support you. Why wait for a crisis or trauma to start the process? Begin your own reshaping today.

Making Your Vision Come Alive

A fun way of getting in touch with what you really want is to make a collage. Gather a few magazines, some of which are new to your perspective, get some paper glue, a poster board, and find a quiet spot. Start by tearing out pictures that appeal to you, then begin gluing them on your poster board. This is just for you; nobody else needs to look at your creation. Because this cutting, tearing, and pasting exercise is reminiscent of kindergarten, you can engage in it with nonlimiting, noncritical abandon. Often, there are very interesting clues in this expansive exercise. When you are finished, step back and take a look. What patterns and themes do you see?

Do you love music? Do you see yourself in the sound, where are you and what are you doing? What dreams does the sound create? While listening, make notes in your journal or record your thoughts in your own voice. You will soon see patterns forming. These patterns will guide you in a creative direction. Music can be very transcendent; it is a direct path to tapping into your creative intuition. Will you be brave enough to follow your own discoveries? Will you be willing to follow them?

Another awareness-raising exercise is automatic or inspirational writing. All you need is pen and paper and a place where you will not be distracted. Begin writing your thoughts down as fast as they come to you; do this without any editing. Do not worry about penmanship or spelling. You will receive a lot of wonderful insights from this exercise. You will get your best results when you repeat this exercise over a period of time. Try doing it three times with at least a day in between. This interval will give you a clean start from the last writing. Each day start fresh with a different type or color of paper, a different pen or pencil, and an open mind.

You might try to write using your nondominant hand. Choose exercises that force you to do usual things in new ways. Using your nondominant hand, whether brushing your teeth or writing, will cause your brain to light up in a completely different pattern. New ideas may be lurking within new styles of thinking, give them a chance to emerge. Give the "Seven favorite things" exercise a try; it is another quick way to tap into

---

Seven favorite things

What gets you up in the morning and drives your energy throughout the day? Your power builds when you put your energy into what is important. Consider your priorities. How does what you normally do compare to what you believe to be important in your life? Complete the following sentence seven times, using different answers. Think of different areas, aspects, and motivations for the use of your energy, money, and time.

I live to:

_____

I live to:

_____

I live to:

_____

I live to:

_____

I live to:

_____

I live to:

_____

I live to:

_____

your vision, if you do it fast and do not edit your thoughts and ideas as you go.

Here is a way to work with your responses. Take a piece of paper.

- ❧ **First**, I would like for you to reorganize your responses so that the most important is listed as #1, and the least important as #7.

- ❧ **Next to each response,** fill in a close estimate of what you consider to be the percentage of the time you now spend doing that activity.

- ❧ **Last**, next to each response, fill in the amount of time you would like to devote to each one. Do not get bogged down in trying to make these percentages add up to exactly 100%; this exercise is to help you gain insight for vision making and goal setting.

By completing these vision-defining exercises, you can develop several pictures of how you want to use your life. This also gives you an opportunity to see more options than you have previously considered and this will broaden your concept of what power is and, consequently, you will build a more expansive life. Think in broad strokes and give some thought to eliminating, adding, and combining views to build a composite picture that truly suits you best.

As you do these exercises, keep in mind that we are multifaceted people with family, friends, work, and hobbies. Include everything; you can crystallize the big picture of your vision later.

What do you see when you read the results from each exercise? What are you saying to yourself? What thoughts seem to be prominent? What similarities do you see, what differences, what inconsistencies are you noticing? Are you giving your power away by not being focused? After you do these exercises, you can better identify your desires and clarify your vision. This can be your first step in gaining control over how you spend your time. And controlling how you use your time is controlling how you use your life.

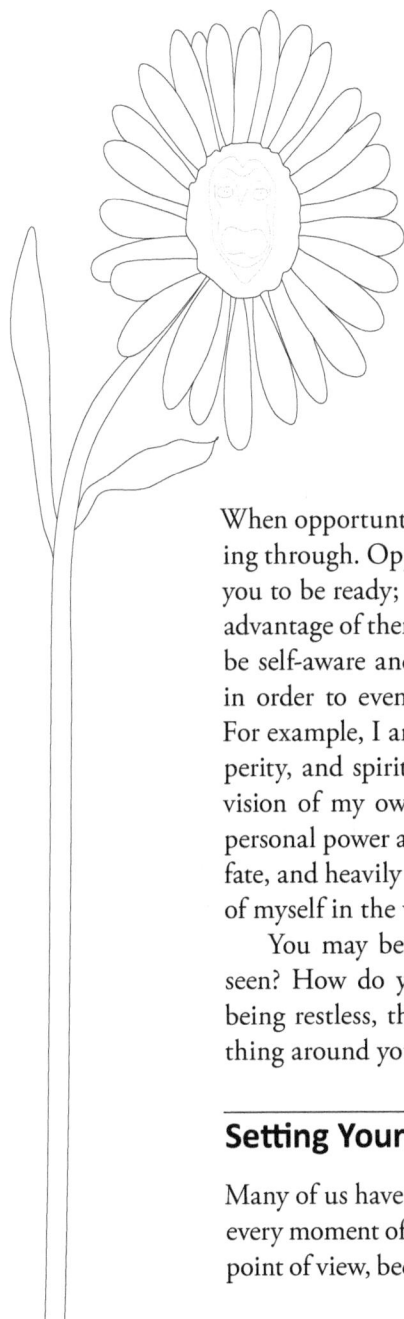

3
Defining Vision
What Do You Want Now?

When opportunties come along, normally they are just passing through. Opportunities never hang around and wait for you to be ready; you must be prepared to grab on and take advantage of them. Consequently, it is imperative for you to be self-aware and purposefully focused on what you want in order to even recognize a small opening of possibility. For example, I am a Life Coach. I focus on happiness, prosperity, and spiritual well-being. If I had not redefined the vision of my own life, I might have continued to believe personal power and abundance were subject to the winds of fate, and heavily dependent on what was happening outside of myself in the world around me.

You may be asking, how do you see what cannot be seen? How do you reach for an unknown? It starts with being restless, then opening your eyes, and noticing everything around you.

Setting Your Priorities

Many of us have bought into the idea that we have to fill up every moment of each day to be successful. I understand this point of view, because I am one of the people whose schedule is divided into 15-minute segments and I can tightly pack each part of my day if I am not aware. There is a perverse badge of honor in being extremely busy. We need relaxation, well-being, and contentment, still, no successful person is a slouch. Even while we are aware of this and reaching for balance and resilience, we know there is more to do, to learn, and to buy everyday. We have barely bought, let alone tackled, one technology before a faster, smarter, cheaper version comes out. It is frustrating to feel we are wasting our time on something that is going to be obsolete very soon. But the simple truth is, everything evolves, from technology, to fashion, to family. Change is a matter of course, and we must choose how we will react to it.

Because we try to pack so much into a day, often we do not access the value of the things we have chosen to do, and the end result of our rushing around is the scattering of our personal energy. If we slow down it is possible to get in sync with the activating essence behind the power of our energy. When this occurs we can see the value of our experience, we can act on our insights, and we are able to invest our time in building essential skills we can use over our lifetime. Making wise choices in what we choose to do sounds simplistic. But it is much more, it has the power to increase our overall happiness. You were not born instinctively knowing how to be successful and create love in an evolving world. This is the reason you need to seek self-knowledge, build your skills, and understand your strengths. The following guidelines will assist you in developing your own personal vision.

Building Your Vision

Start building your vision by deciding how you want to feel when you get what you want. Breathe, relax, and settle into the ease of that feeling now. See it. Live it now. Make it come alive in your imagination. Imagine it; every beautiful building was first seen in someone's imagination before it was constructed, if you can even think of your vision, it is a part of you now. Make that part of you grow, engage the power of purpose, and use your life energy to make yourself great. Your greatness will serve you and others.

These key practices can help in clarifying your vision:

- ❧ Writing down your ideas
- ❧ Being specific
- ❧ Being realistic
- ❧ Being honest in your assessment

Write It Down

Writing sharpens the focus of your intention and takes your ideas into the world of reality. As you write the vision of your life it will become more fully developed, thereby clarifying any fuzziness and creating vivid pictures in your mind. In the beginning you do not have to know how you are going to make it happen. Your own subconscious will look for solutions and options, because you are hard-wired for problem solving. Next time you are presented with a problem, whether embroiled in your kitchen or in international relations, notice how you automatically look for a solution.

You do not have to feel your writing is clear or finished at the first sitting; just keep fleshing out the details of what you want, adding color, smell, and texture. If necessary, let your vision flow and develop, and continue to work out the details over time. When writing, it is vision first, then goals, then tasks, all adding up to one thing: Being prepared for very good timing. Writing helps your vision become seated in your mind and embedded in your desire.

Be Specific

To be reachable, your vision must be specific. How else will you know where you are going? When you aim your mind in a specific clear direction, your subconscious says go for it, make it happen. You need to know exactly what it is you want in order to get it, and when you do get it, you will know you have it.

Do you remember the fables or fairy tales from your childhood, where the genie would grant the hero or heroine a wish, only to have the outcome be not quite what the hero intended? Knowing exactly what you want is very powerful. The next step: be brave and ask for it.

This is where my challenge has been, not asking for enough. Not until I was aware that I was not asking for enough from my life could I begin to muster the power of bravery and start asking. It is like an aha; imagine the forehead slap, first came the realization, "I could be asking for more in my life." Sure, I was leading a good life, but I was just getting up in the morning, exercising, working, and taking care of what needed to be done as it came along. But, realizing I could ask for more, led me to get specific about what I wanted, where I wanted to go, who I wanted to be with, what I wanted to do, and what kind of life I wanted to live. I wanted to walk across Spain, deepen the relationships with my family, and study in France. I wondered, what would happen if I went after those things?

Being specific about what you want can free you, it can untie the threads of a fearful imagination that tethered you to old expectations and fear of the unknown. Fear of an unknown or unexpected future outcome can keep us rooted in the past. I have walked across Spain, studied in

France, reached out to my family, and none of it was exactly as I imagined. When making a decision, sometimes I will think, what unintended results will my actions cause? Maybe they will be larger than what you see, or maybe they will not; however, I do know this: When getting started, it is important for visioning to be as specific as possible and perfect or not, move toward your image anyway.

You will know your vision is specific, and not just a wish, if it is measurable. That means it could be measured by you or any other person. Setting a specific vision may be difficult at first; maybe you can put a number on it and add a time and a date. Maybe you can taste it if you are learning to cook. Setting relationship goals are just the same; they are only different in how you measure them and what you are looking for in each of your relationships. With relationships your measurement of success will be different if you are looking for a romantic companion, or a roommate, or a chess partner. What inherent traits should that person have in order for the relationship to be successful? What is negotiable and not negotiable? How flexible will you be in the relationship? How closely do you match this person, would this person be interested in you? To get the results you want, be clear and be specific.

Be Positive

It has been shown over and over that goals stated positively are far more likely to be met. For that reason, when you set your intention to create an expanded vision of yourself and your future, allow negative thoughts to fall away. Do not push them out forcefully, let them drop, let them dissolve. Visualize yourself as being and living as you want, as if you have already gained your desire. This creates a structural tension within your mind and your subconscious will try to alleviate that tension and create an alignment. Your unconscious mind will automatically engage trying to find a way to achieve what you dream; it will set to work attaining it or changing it. See the box "Tips for thinking positively" for some ideas to help you along the way.

Research has also shown that just practicing looking upward, rather than down, can retrain the mind to be more positive. Your choice of words and how you choose to hold your body have an effect on your attitude. Oscar Wilde observed: "We are all in the gutter, but some of us are looking at the stars." However you choose to approach your vision, it is essential to be active and to be positive.

You are a human being and subject to all the requisite emotions and insecurities, consequently, you are not always going to be in a good mood. If you do your vision planning while you are in a positive mood, it will translate into positive effects and positive results.

Tips for thinking positively

- ❧ Be vigilant with minimizing the negative and accentuating the positive, especially in the way you state your vision. If you make it a habit to speak to yourself positively, you will project positively.

- ❧ If you can remember to be positive with yourself, you can express yourself positively to others as well.

- ❧ When you recognize and cancel a negative thought, replace it with a true and positive one. Be assured, thoughts will slip into your mind. You might as well choose what they are and engage your thinking to work for you.

- ❧ Even if your vision is to eliminate a habit that you consider unhealthy, state your intention positively. For example you might say, "My lungs are healthy, pink, and I breathe deeply to oxygenate my body." Not, "I'm going to quit smoking." Or transform your goal by replacing the bad habit with a positive action that's incongruent with the habit.

- ❧ Spend your time with optimistic people.

Be Realistic

Creating a realistic vision does not mean that what you are building will be easy. Being realistic equates more with being specific. It also means it is attainable and does not reside in the realm of fiction. If you are 55, you may be able to look younger and be a lot healthier, but you cannot be 25 or look 21. If your build is slight, you will not become an NFL linebacker, whatever your age. Think about what David Grayson has said, "All of the discontented people I know are trying sedulously to be something they are not or to do something they cannot do."

This does not mean you cannot set your aim extremely high and go for something very big. Set your vision high. Most people are afraid to set a lofty goal, because they do not how they could possibly accomplish it. Do not worry about the how; the how will work itself out later and the strategies will develop naturally. It works this way because you will start to see opportunities open before you. Your mind will expand, and it will be more flexible and able to work out the details.

Be Sure You Want It

How much do you want the vision you have chosen? This is an important question to ask yourself, because if you have chosen something you only want part way, you will not attain it. You won't. If you have decided you want more time for yourself, but don't know what you would do with the time, you will not get the time. Other people will fill your time for you. Are you comfortable with being partly happy? Are you used to other people making decisions for you? Maybe you are, even so, know that it is possible for you to choose to live a life you love; you may be very close to living powerfully right now.

Set your vision to what you truly want. You go from vision, to goal, to task, not the other way around. As you move through this process, make sure your vision takes effort and is set around the intention that answers three questions:

- ⮞ What do you want?
- ⮞ When do you want it?
- ⮞ Where do you want "it" to happen?

Write your responses to these questions, infuse them with optimism, and then add specific strategies focused on how you will attain these goals. Be sure to include a feasible realistic timeline.

On what areas have you chosen to work? Have you sharpened your focus on them so clearly that you know what you want to accomplish? If you have, you will recognize your achievements, and you will truly know when you are close or complete. When your vision is written down, specific, positive and realistic, it means I could show up with my calendar, watch, calculator, or tape measure and I will know you have succeeded. Or I could speak to your family, friends, and employees and I will know you have quality relationships.

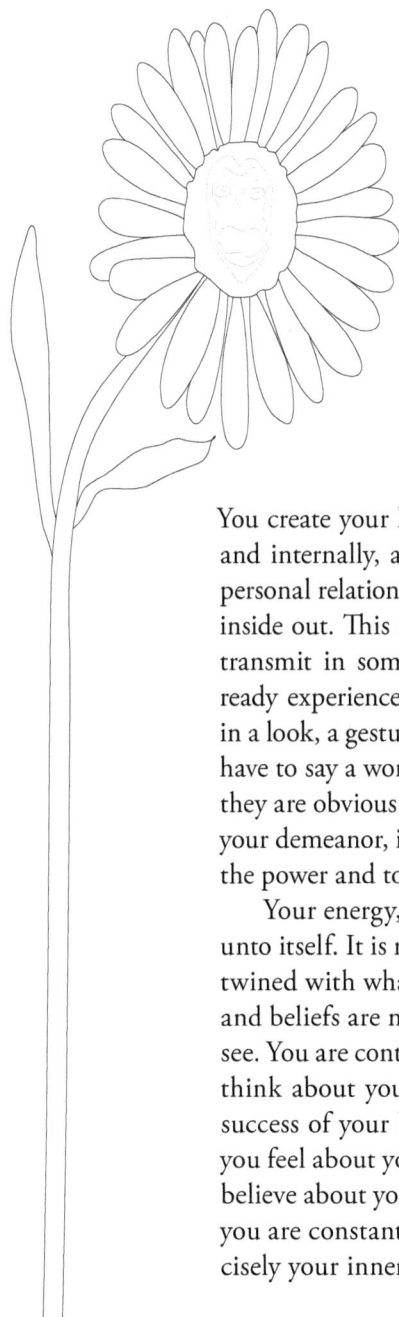

4

Gather Your Energy
You Will Gain Powerful Results

You create your life by everything you tell yourself quietly and internally, and the vitality of your business and your personal relationships are created in the same way, from the inside out. This is because what you think, you will say or transmit in some way to other people. You may have already experienced someone's dislike toward you measured in a look, a gesture, or a chilly silence. That person does not have to say a word to you about his or her feelings, because they are obvious anyway. What you feel is transmitted into your demeanor, it is then projected into how you act and in the power and tone of your voice.

Your energy, whether scattered or focused, is an entity unto itself. It is ruled by the laws of nature and directly entwined with what you believe about yourself. Your energy and beliefs are manifested in your physical body for all to see. You are continually transmitting what you believe and think about yourself and your station, or the status and success of your business to the people around you. What you feel about yourself will become what others think and believe about you, too. This cannot help but happen, since you are constantly broadcasting by numerous avenues precisely your innermost thoughts and feelings.

Analyzing Your Perceptions

As you begin to see everyone and everything as interconnected—not only as human beings but also as energy, mind, and matter—you will realize your core beliefs lead to thought webs that affect your perceptions. If you want to change your perceptions about yourself, your abilities, or your success, change the way you think by becoming more aware of the shifting topography of the mind: A dance of perception, reason, and emotion.

Perceptional changes can be precipitated consciously by the way you choose to think about a situation. Because it is your perceptions that give rise to your emotions, slowing down your thinking process to engage discernment can alter the emotion that emerges. How you perceive yourself or a situation can determine if the same event or human comment will bolster your self-confidence and make you happy, or put you on guard and initiate worry. Your emotions affect your behavior and the actions you choose to take, and the actions you chose will then affect the behavior of the people around you.

You can see how the interconnectedness of our lives, energies, and minds gives rise to the belief that our thoughts can be manifested in the behavior of the people around us. As you begin to take control of the way you think, improve your outlook, and upgrade your behavior, you will feel healthier, do far better, and be more engaged and focused. As a result you will gain positive momentum. I am suggesting that you continue to clarify your core beliefs and make a conscious choice as to which thoughts you pay attention to, and which you let pass by. All thoughts are not equal. If you are able to discern this, you will gain control over your life. Gaining this kind of control will help you build the power and energy to design your life.

Eliminating Energy Drains

Energy drains come disguised in many forms. When you begin to thoughtfully examine them, you will find these include your own self-defeating thoughts and behaviors. You will see fear mongering from the media and governments more clearly. You will know negative and overly critical people for what they truly are. And you will find other people who can be described as energy vampires; they are easily recognized upon reflection. After you have spent time with them, you will feel like you have had the life sucked out of you.

Do not underestimate all of the things that you have left undone; the memory burden of your unfinished tasks will drain your power, sap your energy, and press upon your mind. This stuff becomes a nagging and incomplete personal history that can make you feel like you are dragging around a heavy weight.

Trouble From Within

Trouble does not always come to you as an assault from the outside; sometimes you initiate it from within. You will recognize your internal saboteur because it sounds something like this: "What were you thinking? Why did you say that, you idiot? You can't do that, you've never done it before. People will look at you and laugh." And believe me there are many more things you can say to yourself. They will be targeted, specific, and just perfect for you, because you created them.

If you are aware of your inner saboteur, it will not have the same power over you that it did in the past. Just bringing your awareness to your thoughts, as you berate yourself, helps to neutralize this negative effect. You are not denying your faults, you are just not emphasizing and expanding them. Be consistently kind to yourself by upgrading your personal messages, and accentuating all of the positive things you have built for yourself and done for other people.

Sometimes we have self-limiting beliefs about ourselves, which seem to pop up out of nowhere when nothing has gone wrong. You could be driving or doing the dishes when they catch you by surprise. These are "old idea" habits that are not useful in anything you are creating for yourself today; they get in the way of your purpose, your focus, and your happiness. You are the person taking charge of your dreams and breathing life into them. You are creating both your life and your business from inspiration, from the inside out, and this takes an immense amount of focused energy.

Living your life with high-energy focus is an exciting dynamic way of creating your experience. Old habits will try to seep in, but the longer you can live in powerful creative consciousness, the more you will want it, love it, and live it until it finally becomes a habit. Try living like this, it works both in philosophy and everyday operation; it works because we believe what we consistently live and tell ourselves.

When you are secure in your power and abilities, it will be easier to recognize how gossip and media often exaggerate obscure threats that are rare but very frightening. Bolstering your discernment and resilience in the face of fear from external threats takes consciousness and effort. Yet, if you understand your own mind can exaggerate fear, you can realize many threats are over-rated or purely fictional.

Assaults From the Outside

Sometimes external saboteurs are not easy to spot, and often we confuse them with our internal saboteur. It can be very easy for you to mistake criticism as harsh, jealous, or unreasonable when a friend says something to you to keep you honest and on course. Therefore, it is imperative to learn to trust your gut instincts so that you benefit from them, instead of over reacting to them. Learn to trust those butterflies or the sharp stab in your stomach you sometimes get; your body will tell you what is real and what the truth is now, in the situation you are facing today.

Often the subterfuge is perpetrated by someone who loves you very much. His or her motivations may be buried and unclear. It is possible your loved ones have unconscious fears for your success because they feel they may be left behind as you grow and launch yourself into a new life. Just when you think you are coming into your power and making progress, they will launch into revert-back messages and actions that feel like sabotage. In my experience, your kindness, compassion, and open-heartedness are the only ways to neutralize this situation. Thank them for sharing their concern and stay with your vision.

In business, you may know people who chip away at your self-esteem by being critical or working against you behind your back. This could be someone at any level: your boss, a person who works for you, someone competing for your job, even a person in partnership with you.

Maybe your saboteur is posing as your friend or is your mate. And maybe, the destructive malicious criticism is hard to recognize because it started out slow, built insidiously, and you have become used to it. Whatever your situation is, criticism will weaken your momentum and it can crush your passion for life.

When your self-esteem is being undermined by criticism, eye rolling, and isolation, what is actually happening is the very core of your personal power is being chipped away. You are being attacked. Remember, as you lose your power, you become less creative and less able to make empowered decisions in important areas of your life. If this is happening to you, fortunately, you can take steps toward putting yourself back together and keeping it that way.

Choosing Powerful Solutions

How you react to inevitable verbal and nonverbal assaults either creates or depletes your personal power. It is part of your life's journey to learn how to deal with difficult people, that is why we all know them. Only a small glimpse of such a person can still repel me. The smirk, the swagger, the tone of voice, or the haughty laugh, any one of these can trigger a memory of a past offense to cause an old wound to fester, and freeze my compassion and reason. Yet reacting like that is not a powerful response. When dealing with assaults from an external saboteur, stay with your vision and purpose and go through the following process.

- **First**, do not overreact. Take a breath. Slow down and simply feel the physical sensations in your body. Meditate on them. What gut intuitions are you receiving from the criticism or feedback? What are you resisting? These physical sensations are speaking to you; notice them.

- **Next**, ask yourself, is it possible to see this person as a human being, as wanting the same thing for his or her life as you want, happiness, meaning, and bravery? Is it possible to see this person as coming from the same creation as you? If you can, you may be able to feel what it is like to be in the other person's skin.

- **Then**, ask yourself, do your gut reactions match your thoughtful assessment of the situation? Are you seeing the bigger picture, or are you judging the person, the person's actions, and the situation through the lenses of your own desires and weaknesses? Have you developed a fixed image of your friend or business associate?

- **Last**, it is time to carefully choose your reaction to the input you are receiving from your perceived saboteur. Have you truly felt the sting of betrayed intimacy? Have you interpreted the situation accurately? Ask for help if necessary; however, only you can decide what you think and how you will proceed.

Not all relationships are created equal; one is not always as good as another. In fact, maintaining a bad relationship will not only leave you less time for good ones, it will drive them away. When you present your idea, a good friend may point out a couple of flaws you do not see. But beware, as soon as you hear your friend giving nothing but excuses for why your idea will not work, see this as a red flag in the relationship.

During the introspective phase of choosing your reaction to a saboteur, carefully decide which choices will build your power and enable you to create a more satisfying life for yourself, your family, and your community, and design a life that expands this intent and the world around you.

When you slow your thinking down enough to make an empowered decision, rather than a choice made from the weakened state of eroded self-esteem, you will create a much more desirable consequence. It seems a simple thing, yet making a choice and living with the consequence is exactly what we work with every day; it is difficult and no small accomplishment to manifest your inspiration into physical form. Achieving this requires a tremendous amount of energy and focus. Be careful, choose wisely, and do not be too quick to give away your precious energy.

Recognizing and Completing the Past

The work seems so clear; of course you want to make choices from a position of power. Yet before you have the energy to continually activate powerful choices, you need to continue to eliminate energy drains. You do this by acknowledging your history and doing what it takes to complete what is past. If you have your attention tied up with a myriad of unfinished things, you do not have the energy to live for today, let alone any energy for the future. Your power is tethered to the past.

It is no surprise that you do not have the energy to do what it takes to move forward if you hold grudges, live and work in clutter, or have made promises you have not kept. How could you possibly keep your attention on the pleasures of today and build a future, when you are profusely bleeding energy every day? If you are not getting what you want, here is how to get unstuck and live your life by design.

These are the basic steps:

- ❧ Finish unfinished business.
- ❧ Clear a path by cutting through the clutter.
- ❧ Express your thanks.
- ❧ Choose forgiveness.

Unfinished Business

Energy is your electricity. Now imagine there is a string of energy running like a wire from you to each thing you have left unfinished. When you have that much leakage, it is difficult to build a reservoir of strength. If you promised six months ago to copy and send an article to a colleague, send it. If you do not send it, call that person and tell him or her you are not going to send the article and be finished with it. Remember the lunch you have wanted to have with a friend you miss and do not see enough, call and schedule that too. Either do or eliminate all of those things, no matter how small they seem to you.

It is impossible to add anything new to your life, whether it is more prized possessions or possibilities, when you have attachments to your unfinished business. This is because new incomplete tasks merely pile onto the old. If you have developed the habit of not finishing things, it will only get worse if you do not clear it up now. When you have made promises and have not kept them, guilt creeps in, nags you, and undermines your focus. Guilt erodes happiness and will create nothing except more worry and regret.

Clearing a Path

A lot of stuff clutters our lives, from the mail that arrives every day, to gifts, and objects we bought impulsively years ago. Our homes, cars, and offices are all spaces just waiting to get filled up, and they do. Each thing we hang on to and do not use holds old energy. Clothes we used to wear but now no longer fit us, only take up space and terrorize us from our closets. Pass them on while they are still in style: someone will use them now and you will feel better about your gift. (Also see tips on developing your personal style in Chapter 9.)

After you go through your closets, check your kitchen drawers and your filing cabinets. One of my clients had old divorce records; another had pounds of files on vehicles he no longer owned. I had manuals on products tossed out long ago. What useless things are you holding on to? "Clutter professionals" advise a three-way approach when beginning to tackle clutter, whether it is one drawer or one room. Take everything out and divide into three piles: keep it, give it away, throw it away, but do what works for you. Clearing out can be very difficult to do because we see value in the objects and we know what we spent to obtain them. In fact, the stuff can almost look like money. But what is the true cost of keeping things we do not use or need? This is the question each of us must answer for ourselves.

When we begin to notice how the stuff in our lives requires our attention, we begin to see how much of our power we are placing into those things. We have to find a place for the object, clean it, maintain it, and live with it. It can be like establishing a relationship.

Yet at the same time, our photographs, sacred heirlooms, and many things we collect connect us to a positive past. They remind us of a history we want to remember and integrate into our present lives. These are the possessions that have meaning to us. If that is the case, we need to keep them. However, there are many more items that just take up space. When we remove those things and create more space in our lives, then energeti-

29

cally we have room for the new and bright to enter, the objects that allow us to live the present. Maybe we will even have room to breathe.

Who Needs Your Thanks?

Even though I feel we are all energetically connected, at the same time our interpersonal connections are tenuous at best. Even people we have known all of our lives do not instinctively know the depth of our feelings or gratitude. This is true for everyone in nearly all of our relationships, from business associates to our closest loved ones. Each one of us says we want deeper, more meaningful relationships, yet sometimes we withhold even the most meager expressions of gratitude. We need to thank others in ways they find meaningful and are easy to interpret. To whom do you owe an acknowledgement? Go deliver it; be magnanimous and tell other people how well they are doing. Remember, "A thankful heart is not the greatest virtue, but the parent of all virtues."—Cicero

Being grateful and expressing it has more significance than it first seems. This very act opens your heart and mind and enables you to receive more in your life. Gratitude is an exchange of energy that empowers both the giver and the recipient. Everyone wants to know his or her efforts are appreciated. Also, it is just as important to gracefully accept honest appreciation, because gratitude works both in the giving and the receiving to release resentment and in opening the mind and the heart. Expressing gratitude creates meaningful interactions and activates deep communication between people on an intuitive level. When I delivered and read aloud a letter describing precise thankfulness to my parents, they were deeply and genuinely moved. I am not sure who received most from this significant interaction, yet not knowing is part of gratitude's wonder. What I do know is that the expression of gratitude brought closeness, and added joy and energy to our relationship.

When you are filled up with thankfulness and appreciation, there is room for generosity to spill out. Generosity in and of itself is a powerful dynamic energy. It connects you with other people, even those who were not the direct recipients of your gifts. Generosity activates flow in both money and creativity, and being in flow is very close to transcendence and enlightenment. When you are in life's flow, you become authentically generous, and when true generosity is activated you become more insightful and intuitive.

About Forgiveness

Forgiveness is a tricky issue, because it is difficult to understand the energetic dynamics involved around the whole idea of forgiving. Forgiveness is not about bestowing or granting redemption and being right. It is about freedom and consciousness. Also, there are untold types of hurts and transgressions. Many times the grievances are minor; however, sometimes the hurt may be deep and ongoing. When you make the choice to forgive, you need not make the choice to forget. There is always an important life lesson in what you have experienced, and maybe you need to protect yourself.

But, choosing to hold a grudge means you must divert a significant amount of energy, and focus it on the grievance or the person in general. Your rancor can easily degenerate into resentment and settle into bitterness, if you allow this to happen, it will be you who suffers. Think how tragic this is, especially when the grievance turns out to be a mere misunderstanding. Choosing to stay truly conscious through the process of forgiving will enable you to learn from the experience. This also allows you to release your locked up personal power, reclaim it, and use it wisely. I particularly like how Jack Kornfield expresses this, "Forgiveness is primarily for our own sake, so we no longer have to carry the burden of resentment. But to forgive does not mean we allow injustice in again."

Who are you holding in a static state of built-up grievances? Is it an ex-spouse, a neighbor, an old friend, maybe even your parents? What was your complicity in forming the grudge? Everyone changes; you have changed, and you have learned and grown. Do yourself and others the favor of releasing your old and tired solid perceptions. Do you really want to use your life force to hold every thing steady? Can you really do that anyway? Wouldn't it be wiser to let your energy flow?

Ancient wisdom from the Bhagavad Gita tells us, "If you want to see the brave look at those who forgive."

Forgiving people is a journey into courage, because then you can no longer give another person's behavior the power to keep you where you are in life. You are then responsible for your own behavior and that is very scary. Use your power of awareness to consciously let go of your grudges, and you will notice that your choices and decisions will be initiated from a stronger more loving position. When you forgive, it is you who will feel lighter and freer.

Many volumes have been written about the energetic dynamics of forgiveness. People are so much more than the confined narrow parameters in which we view them. We make judgments about a person who has wronged us and then judge their every act or word negatively. This keeps us locked in our present state of limited options. Withholding forgiveness inhibits our ability to move on and build more for ourselves. Do not get locked in place. Forgiveness is an act of will that starts with a decision, and you can use your will power to open the flow of forgiveness now. Ask yourself, are you ready to do this?

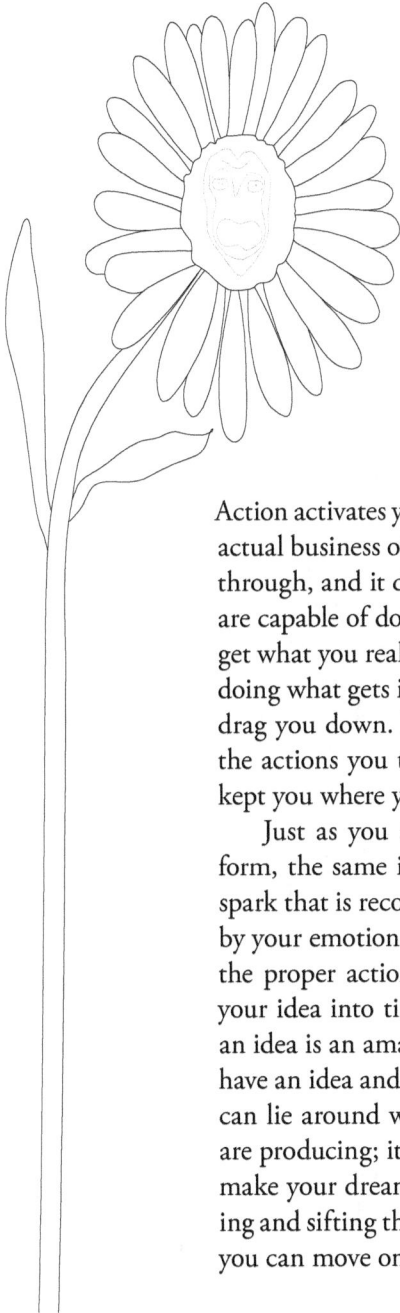

5

Taking Action

From Believing to Following Through

Action activates your power and is the key to success. It is the actual business of believing, planning, doing, and following through, and it distinguishes the living from the dead. You are capable of doing more or changing what you do now to get what you really want. Maybe your action will be to stop doing what gets in your way, or stop being with people who drag you down. Hope and optimism in combination with the actions you take will get you over any inertia that has kept you where you are in life.

Just as you are a spark of the divine manifested into form, the same is true for your idea. It starts as a creative spark that is recognized in your mind and after that carried by your emotions to your body. Then it is up to you to take the proper action and do the work necessary to manifest your idea into time and space, the material world. Having an idea is an amazing conceptual leap, yet it is one thing to have an idea and another to bring that idea into reality. You can lie around when you are dreaming, but not when you are producing; it takes an incredible shift in your energy to make your dream come alive in the physical world. Accepting and sifting through your doubts, fears, and hopes so that you can move on is a heroic part of your human journey.

Making the Most of Today

You are reading this book because you have decided to make changes in how you live life; you would like to be happier, to have better relationships, or live with economic security. You will accomplish this by living fully present today and focusing forward, not on what is behind you. These changes require action; therefore, you cannot continue to do things the way you have always done them. If you do, you are still living in the past. I am not suggesting you forget your history, but think of situations where you have already received inspirations and did not do anything with them. Have you ever been in a meeting and had a great idea but kept quiet, then someone else had the same idea, but spoke up and got all of the credit? This is merely a simple example; however you can extrapolate this out to the important decisive moments in your life and understand the far-reaching impact. It is imperative that you take action, because without taking the appropriate action, inspiration leads only to the frustration of wondering what could have been. If you choose not to act, then where will you be; will you be worse off?

Unplugging From Fear and Self-Doubt

Fear kills dreams, gets in the way, and can stop you dead in your tracks. Everyone is susceptible to self-doubt, no one is immune. It is how you react to the doubt once it arises that makes a difference. Fear of failure and inertia can keep you from implementing your ideas and undermine your good intentions. As you begin to make your dreams a reality, you begin to experience resistance. Doubt and fear are pressures so intense and adept they have stopped many people from making their ideas come alive in the physical realm. Remember, "Fear is a trick, a sham, a sleight of hand. It is an illusion."—Emmanuel

This is the point in which a plethora of excuses will once again come flooding into your mind. Unplug from the doubt by putting structures into place that you can easily use when you do not feel like doing the necessary work. Each person is plagued by doubt—this includes both the successful and the struggling—the only difference between them is that the successful do the work anyway.

Experiencing Winning

Most people would rather complain than do what it takes to get what they yearn for most. In fact, they even complain to people who cannot do anything about the mess in their life. Winning means clearing away any obstacles in your way, rather than tying up your energy in trying to avoid the hindrance. The act of going toward something is totally different than running away from something. If you set your focus on an object or a concept you are pulled toward it. When this happens choice engages and you can decide whether you will move toward your vision or not. If you decide to go for it, it means you will need to stop complaining and then take responsibility to make things happen. Conversely, if you are running away from something you are engaging fear, and paradoxically you will draw to you precisely what you are trying to repel. What you resist continues to persist because that is where you place your focus.

Character traits of winners

Think about it: people who win and people who do not, have the same fears and doubts. Winners are people who do the things that other people do not want to do. When you make a move you cause things to happen: your action always creates a reaction. What actions are you going to take and what traits are you going to cultivate?

- ⮞ They have people who support them. Friends or family members can act as an antidote to toxic people, who are everywhere in your life. Winners have limited the number of flawed relationships they will endure and they also develop fewer but deeper relationships.

- ⮞ They have someone to coach them. Everyone needs a mentor. This is a person you admire and on whom you can call when you need to ask questions. Look for someone in your professional organization or hire a coach.

- ⮞ They are responsible for themselves. This means taking responsibility for their lives and the decisions they have made. They have stopped complaining and blaming other people for what they do not have.

Taking Courage and Being Positive

The present moment is where the power of your energy rests. This is where all action resides; action always takes place in the present moment, not in the past or the future. Decide consciously to take action, because even small positive active changes will enhance your experience of the present and alter the possibilities for your future. Consequently, I encourage you to notice what you think and initiate the process of throwing out all of your self-limiting thoughts and behaviors, then begin to replace them immediately with positive thoughts, plans, and actions.

I know, this is a major directive, replacing everything negative with the positive is not a superficial exercise. It pierces deep into your unconscious, and you will begin to see how often fear, worry, and negativity take over your thoughts. Even though it may not seem so when you are coming face-to-face with fault after fault, doing this supports your progress to living more happily. Remember, you are not denying your shortcomings; you are accentuating what you do well.

Being positive connects you with others and to the true power of your being. Choosing to be positive and powerful increases your opportunity for achieving happiness and a high level of success, this is because being positive activates a seductive energy that draws people to you. They want to help you and be part of a success system. Success is contagious and people inherently recognize a flourishing person and naturally gravitate to him or her.

In the past I have said, "Wherever you are, begin, just start, get up and go," and I still suggest this. However, I have a caveat, it is important for you to understand that action is a powerful process and it is vital for you to seriously consider what you choose to activate. You can activate a field of grace by consciously and intentionally choosing positive thought and action. Conversely, if you choose to see people as cheats, liars, and as being deceitful, the actions you choose will be developed to fulfill your perceptions. It can be said that you can activate the sacred or the profane, and you can be a conduit for either.

Practicing Persistence

Many of you may be building businesses that no person has ever conceived of before. You may be thinking of new ways to energize the world, and you may have set out to create something so new no model for success exists yet. During the process you are going to experience disappointment while you work out the new structures. This will happen even if you are merely learning to use new equipment or developing new relationship styles. When you encounter this inevitable disappointment, you can use your experience as an opportunity to be patient with yourself and practice persistence.

During the development phase of your project you are going to try a lot of things that may not work out. If you can view each activity as a learning experience, you can choose to view it as a success even though it may not seem to be. When your efforts appear to be less than successful, you have merely discovered something that did not work. Along the way you will find many options that do work and work well, and you will build upon these successes in ways that will stretch your imagination and build your confidence.

When you find success along the way, celebrate it. Congratulate yourself, make a big deal of it, even have a party. Always stop and pause a moment before charging ahead, in order to feel the underlying joy of your persistence. Always remember, there are many times along the route from the inspiration of an idea, to the manifestation of your dreams, that the entire process can be aborted. Will you be one of the many people who apply the brakes when things get tough, or one of the few who persevere?

Adding Consistency

"We are what we repeatedly do. Excellence then, is not an act but a habit." Through his statement, we can see that Aristotle understood the importance of consistency. If you realize that you are becoming frustrated by the changes you are implementing, your rate of progress, or with any new project you are planning, remember that consistency in your behavior will build a steady habit and it will keep your success and creativity flowing. Keep these ideas in mind:

- **First**, stop poking at the beehive of negative beliefs that swarm up in an instant in your mind.

- **Next**, shield yourself from naysayers who are waiting in line to tell you in several different ways that you are wasting your time.

- **Last**, do not be discouraged by failure; rarely has an invention or innovation worked on the first attempt. Your consistency, not your frenzied efforts, will be the key to your success.

Learn to cultivate the qualities of courage, persistence, and consistency; they have the ability to support you throughout your life, as well as sustain you on your journey to success. Also, using proven time-management and self-management skills can help you in the areas of consistency and perseverance. If you acquire these skills. you can use them to ease your workload, not to pile more work onto you. (Chapters 6 and 7 will assist you in building those skillls.) Any time you begin to feel overwhelmed, do not speed up, slow down, take a walk, or run, do yoga, and breathe deeply. A change of perspective will give you a chance to pause, gather your strength, and center your energy. Then see that you are capable, and know that you are continually surrounded by hope, options, and divinity.

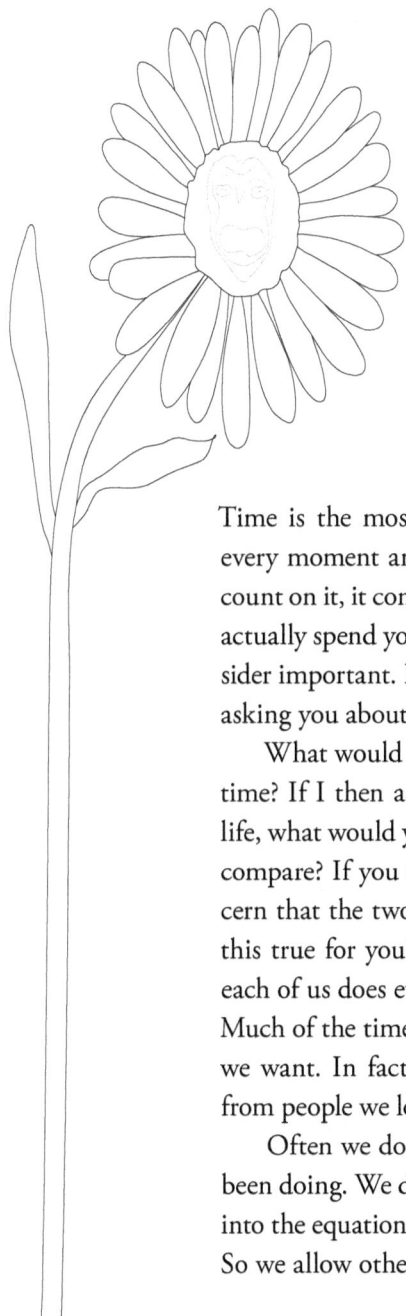

6

Where Does the Time Go?

Using the Power of Time to Get What You Want

Time is the most valuable asset you have. Time exists in every moment and even as we try to hold it, count it, and count on it, it continually slips away. Consequently, how you actually spend your time says a lot about what you truly consider important. Did you answer the questions in Chapter 2 asking you about how you spend your time?

What would you say if I asked you how you spend your time? If I then asked you, what is most important in your life, what would your response be, how would those answers compare? If you are like most people, it is very hard to discern that the two responses came from the same person. Is this true for you? If it is, you are not alone. Most of what each of us does every day does not reflect our true priorities. Much of the time what we do does not get us closer to what we want. In fact it fragments our power and separates us from people we love.

Often we do what we do, because that is what we have been doing. We do not consider how all of our actions factor into the equation of a happy, successful, and meaningful life. So we allow others to fill up our schedules, and we do tasks that could be eliminated. Also, we do things that we could have hired other people to do more effectively and a lot more efficiently.

Do you fill up your schedule and keep very busy, so you can put off looking at your life and put off making hard decisions about your time? I know I have done this. However, at any time it can be different. If you pause long enough to evaluate where your time goes, you can become aware of its value and you can begin to pull the fragments of your energy back together, and harness the power of time.

Learning How Long Tasks Take

Commonly we over or under estimate the time it takes to do things, even routine tasks and the things we do every day. For example, it takes less than 10 seconds to file several folders, but how many times have you procrastinated doing simple tasks because you thought it would take too long? In the time it takes to heat up a cup of water in the microwave, you can take the trash out or wipe down the counter. Do not underestimate the power of very small segments of time. They are significant and meaningful and add up to make a powerful difference in the quality of life. How long does it take to flash someone a smile or jot a note of gratitude?

When it comes to allotting time for work, one of our biggest mistakes is forgetting to allow time for interruptions or the necessity of reworking a plan. We also underestimate the amount of time it will take to do the research required before we even start the project. Always factor in time for interruptions, restructuring, and research. Because of these reasons it would be wiser to recalculate your time estimates for finishing a job upwards by at least 25%.

However, the real question is, how are you spending your precious time? What are you doing with the 168 hours you receive every week? I am sure you have some idea; still, we are not very good observers of our own behavior. In fact, we tend to be very unreliable when asked to estimate our own time allocations. Consequently, we need a system to help us observe and record our behavior.

Before you can reallocate your time you first need to truly know how you use your time, not just your best guess. Remember, do not trust your estimates; collect reliable figures. After you gather this data, you will receive two benefits.

First, you will be able to see if you are spending your time the way you want to be spending it. Second, after you have made more effective use of your available time, you will be able to judge the usefulness of your changes. These are very simple concepts, but understanding them could be crucial, quite momentous, and give you a big piece of your life back. Of course you have to be brave and willing to honestly look at your life.

Recording and Categorizing Your Time

I have chosen two distinctly different methods for tracking how you use your time. For best results choose a normal workday and a normal off day to compare the differences and similarities in your behavior. If none of your days are normal, then pick a couple of days at random.

24-Hour Schedule

Begin tracking your time and actions, add start and stop times, and list exactly what you are doing. Then categorize each activity you do into groups, using the categories: shared, private, work, and project time. This method is the more involved of the two, yet it is still very simple. It helps to color code your activities for a fast visual assessment of how you are using your time. You can go back with different colored highlighters and highlight sections accordingly. I have suggested colors at the end of each group; however, feel free to change the colors and choose ones that have more meaning or significance for you:

- **Shared time**: time that you spend with people with whom you are intimate, your family, and very close friends. (Pink)

- **Private time**: time you set aside for yourself, to be with friends, meditate, read, or whatever you chose. (Yellow)

- **Work time**: time you spend working on all aspects of your job. Include travel time, preparation time, or getting dressed, everything it takes to get you working inside or outside your home. (Green)

- **Project time**: time you spend on projects, home improvements, classes, sports, or crafts. (Blue)

30-Minute Schedule

Using this method you keep track of what you do every 30 minutes. Set your watch or a timer for 30 minutes. When it rings set it for another 30 minutes, and so forth throughout the day. It sounds tedious but the coding is simple; chart where you are and what you do during each of these 30-minute intervals. Then, go back over your chart.

- Highlight with green every activity or 30-minute interval that you think brings you closer to your vision.

- Highlight with yellow all of the activities you chose to do and found joyful, stimulating, or restful.

What surprises do you see in your schedule? Are you squandering your time? Are the people you love receiving your time, or do you give your time away too readily to others less significant to you? What activities are left in your schedule, what is not highlighted? What were you doing then? What do you want to add? what do want to stop doing? Most likely you can make minor adjustments and start getting very positive results.

Starting Where You Are

Perhaps you have found that you are not living the life you want to live because you are not doing the things that are important to you. Then where you are right now is the right place to start using your time in ways that are more significant. Do not worry about what you have missed, let it be, as there is a whole lot more to come. Nothing will be gained if you live in sadness and regret worrying about lost time. Start building more power in your life from where you are now at this moment.

No starting point can be too humble and no step too small, because you cannot wish yourself to have more money, an education, or love. Moreover, you already know just more time passing will not give you what you want. It is easy to feel you are in over your head and what you are doing is too difficult. When you feel overwhelmed, and a project seems too formidable, back up a little bit, or stop, then take smaller steps. Sometimes you have merely tried to do too much at once or you have started the project before you have properly organized it.

If you feel overwhelmed, a good remedy to get you going is to divide your larger vision into several independent intermediate goals. By doing this you will add more joy and energy to your vision, be able to create more-manageable steps, and lessen the angst and stress that builds from what can feel like endless effort. Each day of life is a precious gift; do not waste what today has to offer because of a narrow focus on attainment. How you treat today is how you will treat tomorrow. I have found it helps to write out each step as a specific, positive, and realistic but smaller vision of its own. This paced step-wise method of achievement is a great motivator because it gives you the opportunity to celebrate many small wins. In turn, achieving and celebrating honors the little child in you that loves to be rewarded. Do not ignore the child aspect of your personality; it is an important playful presence in each one of us.

Just like with any larger vision, you go through the same process of constructive planning when you start these smaller sections too. Then take the appropriate actions immediately and consistently. When you divide up the work, you can see big chunks of your vision being completed and these intermediate wins help you feel positive with your progress. And when you're positive, it is more likely you will live your vision. Success leads to success and being rewarded consistently helps build that reality.

A lot happens in this world and in your life that is completely out of your control. It would be simplistic for me to imply you control the behavior of others, or whether or not you contract an illness. This is not within the realm of human influence. You also know it to be true, that if anyone stops you from getting what you want out of your life, it will probably be you. Most likely, although not always, your biggest enemy is yourself and what you allow into your life. So step forward, organize your behavior and your thinking to allow inspiration to enter your life. It is when you allow inspiration to enter, that then, you can do what it takes to be powerful and to live the life of your vision.

Please do not be intimidated by the time it will take to accomplish your vision, to complete your education, or even to complete the task you are doing right now. This wisdom has been known for centuries, Confucius, from the 5th century BC said, "It does not matter how slow you go so long as you do not stop." Time is ineffable, sometimes it appears to slow down, and other times it appears to speed up. Whatever our perception, time continues to pass anyway; what matters is how we use the passing time. Managing your time is within the sphere of your influence. Begin today to maximize the quality of your time. Take this step; it is entirely within your control.

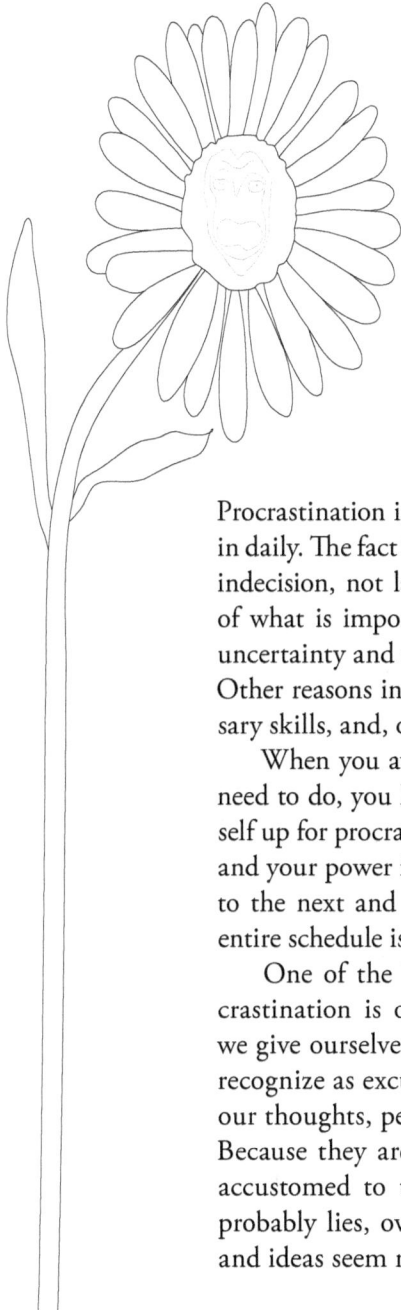

7

Living Time, Not Killing Time

Going from Procrastination to Problem Solving

Procrastination is one of the biggest time killers we engage in daily. The fact is most of the time delays are initiated from indecision, not laziness. People often do not have a sense of what is important. In the moment of action they fear uncertainty and are confused about what needs to be done. Other reasons include a lack of confidence, a lack of necessary skills, and, of course, a desire to avoid unpleasantness.

When you avoid or put off doing what you know you need to do, you know it, and on some level, you beat yourself up for procrastinating as a result, procrastination grows and your power fails. One undone or unfinished task leads to the next and then the next. Before you know it, your entire schedule is in total chaos.

One of the biggest impediments to overcoming procrastination is our inability to see through the excuses we give ourselves. These stories are sometimes difficult to recognize as excuses, because they automatically pop into our thoughts, permeate our minds, and appear to be true. Because they are so pervasive and insidious, we become accustomed to telling ourselves these same old excuses, probably lies, over and over until the same old thoughts and ideas seem normal.

Old stories can become unchallenged excuses, and these hindrances are always detrimental in your effort to change your life or to overcome procrastination. When you examine your old stories you may find you have outgrown them, or that they were never true in the first place. At that time, when you see clearly how you have grown, you will be able to write new stories for yourself.

Common excuses for procrastination

What are your personal excuses? Have you heard yourself use any of these? Which stories do you use, and what other excuses can you add to the list?

- ❧ I'm too busy with my day-to-day work to tackle anything new.
- ❧ I'll start tomorrow.
- ❧ I don't know how to do it.
- ❧ It's not going to take that long, so I'll do some other things first.
- ❧ I'm too tired.
- ❧ It's not really that important.

I, too, understand these excuses. Sometimes, when I am relaxing, I have to literally order myself out of the chair I am sitting in, just to finish a task that could have already been completed. Excuses are common to human behavior, even if the job is a little thing that takes only 30 seconds or 5–10 minutes. Other times we lie to ourselves and we do not even know it. We tell ourselves we are not smart enough or creative enough. Each one of us is vulnerable to delaying excuses, but we do not have to be anymore.

We Are All Creative People

Human beings are truly a creative species; we have survived without fur or sharp teeth or claws. By necessity our survival has depended on creativity and ingenuity, because this is true you and I are here today. Since you have descended from people who found creative ways to gather food, or to hide and hunt, you have inherited those creative genes. Your ancestors were a part of communities that built civilizations, and you are descended from them: You cannot help but be creative.

Creativity is a spontaneous energy that powers our body and our minds. In turn, we are empowered by the way creativity flows through us. Creativity helps us to solve problems and it pushes out procrastination by adding vitality. It is an antidote for stress and depression; rarely are we happier than when we are channeling creativity. If we quiet our bodies and minds when vulnerability arises, peace can enter, and we become capable of channeling energetic creativity for powerful recuperative results.

Each of us is capable of tapping into our creativity and making it an integral and potent part of our lives, if we give ourselves the space to let it happen. When we view ourselves as uncreative, we deny an entire aspect of our personalities and inhibit our growth.

At the other extreme, sometimes highly creative people can tend to spend large amounts of energy on one area of their lives and then be totally depleted in others. This distorted type of energy allocation leads to a lack of mindfulness, clutter accumulation, and life imbalance, and balance in all areas is necessary for health, happiness, and prosperity.

Maintaining balance in our lives requires ongoing effort, and mounting clutter can throw us totally out of whack. One of the ways I have found to help me with this is to set aside 5 minutes each hour to clean off my desk, counter, or whatever cluttered work station or surface I have found myself toiling on or around. Either clear it off completely or do just one small part of it. You will be surprised at how much you can get done in just one 5-minute period. At the end of the week you will see a lot of improvement, and at the end of 2 weeks, I promise you will be genuinely satisfied with the results you create.

Problem-Solving Skills

You truly want your vision; it is fixed, written, specific, and clear. You have cleared your space, scheduled your time, built your enthusiasm, and even been "less negative." Yet the relationship, the clients, or the money, have not started pouring in the way you imagined. Now it is time to focus on the actual strategy you need to implement, and the actions you need to take to make what you want a living reality. Look at your abilities, where you are, and what you have. As Theodore Roosevelt said, "Do what you can, with what you have, where you are."

When I applied the Seven Effective Problem-Solving Steps that you will find on the next page to my attempts at losing weight, I began to see results. I knew I ate nutritious food and I walked every day. So, why does every camera have a distorted lens and it seems someone is stepping on the scale with me? It was becoming obvious; the gorgeous reflection in the mirror and the photographs of me were incongruent. I decided to ask the

Seven effective problem-solving steps

Following the steps in the exercise below can help you overcome inertia and procrastination. You will find this exercise more effective when you write your answers out, because writing helps to crystallize your thoughts and to firmly seat your desire.

1. State your vision once again. Restate what you want and where you want to be using clear, precise, and succinct language to describe your dream. Again, set a time frame in which you want to achieve it.

2. Look at where you are, right now, and be honest about your starting point. It will help you choose the proper route to take. Write this down too.

3. Brainstorm several different options or avenues to reach your vision. There are many paths to attaining your dreams. Use this time to examine all of them. Let your ideas fly, without editing yourself, and write them all down. Then list each option, and write it out individually.

4. Choose only one of these options. Pick the one option that looks like the best. If you try too many avenues you will dilute your effort and get distracted. When you are side-tracked, you lessen your chances of attaining your dream.

5. Define specifically the method you chose. Now fully describe the option you chose in a way that is so clear, that not only you but other people can easily understand your choices and the actions you will take in the pursuit of your vision.

6. Do the work this method takes. Schedule a time to start your work, and then schedule time each day to implement the work you need to do.

7. Evaluate your success. How will you define success? Decide now, so you can compare your idea of success with your actual results at the end of the journey. Success can end up looking as if it slides along a continuum, and you will want to evaluate your results effectively.

question, what am I missing? I thought I was doing it right, yet not getting results. When I took an honest look, the truth appeared. I walked nearly every day and mostly ate good nutritious foods. What I needed to do was make some small but significant changes to receive different results. Do not be fooled because you have it 80%–90% figured out. That last 10%-20% will make all the difference in what you get in this world. Your happiness and success are at stake. Start today, and take the necessary steps to work through your obstacles.

I am convinced a lot of us are very close to living the life we want. When you clarify your focus you magnify your power, then it is possible for you to naturally attract what you want. If this is the where you are having trouble and you cannot identify what you need to change, it is located in your blind spot. Now is the time to reach out for help; ask friends to tell you are what you are missing, hire a coach, and pay attention to your dreams. Clues are left in the wake of your actions, take a look, what do you see? You will notice hints in repeating patterns and see more in the guise of annoyances. Once you do identify those small changes you need to make, consistently put in the effort and time, you will crack the code to success.

Tipping Points

At first you may see very poor results from the changes in your thinking and the actions you are taking. This is the point many people give up, because the results have been so meager compared to their efforts. However if you keep at it, there will come a time that you cross over an invisible line. At that point, with only slightly more effort, you will begin to see dramatic results from your accumulated work. At the moment you cross over the invisible line, you have crossed the tipping point.

This concept can easily be seen in the amortization schedule of a home mortgage. In the beginning only a tiny fraction of your payment goes to paying the principle on the loan. Most of your payment is interest and goes directly to the bottom line of the bank. If you are paying only a regular payment, it will be years, maybe decades, before you reach the tipping point. But when you do cross that line, the payment toward the principle of your mortgage accelerates quickly. As you work toward your vision, you will cross the tipping point also. Then you will see your dreams materialize and the ease with which you slip into your personal power accelerates too.

Sticking to a Stopping Time

Sometimes the hardest thing to do is to stop work, when you have worked your allotted amount of time. You might think you will just work another

5 minutes, but 5 minutes will turn into a half an hour and even longer. Set a stopping time and when you have reached that prearranged amount of work time, stop and stick with it. When you stop working, stop completely, and relax actively. Take your mind off the one more thing you could have done. Tell yourself that you are off duty and that you will resume your work at your next scheduled work time. If this is difficult to do, look at this as a promise you are keeping to yourself, honor yourself as you would a good friend. As this practice becomes a habit, it becomes a relief to know you can count on having free time.

If you have a good idea when you are "off duty," write it down and implement it when you are scheduled to work. Your off time is just as important as the work you do. Because you are using your brain and body in different ways, you will accomplish much more when you are working and you will avoid burnout. Choose to relax; it revitalizes you and recharges your outlook. In fact, without rest, work is impossible.

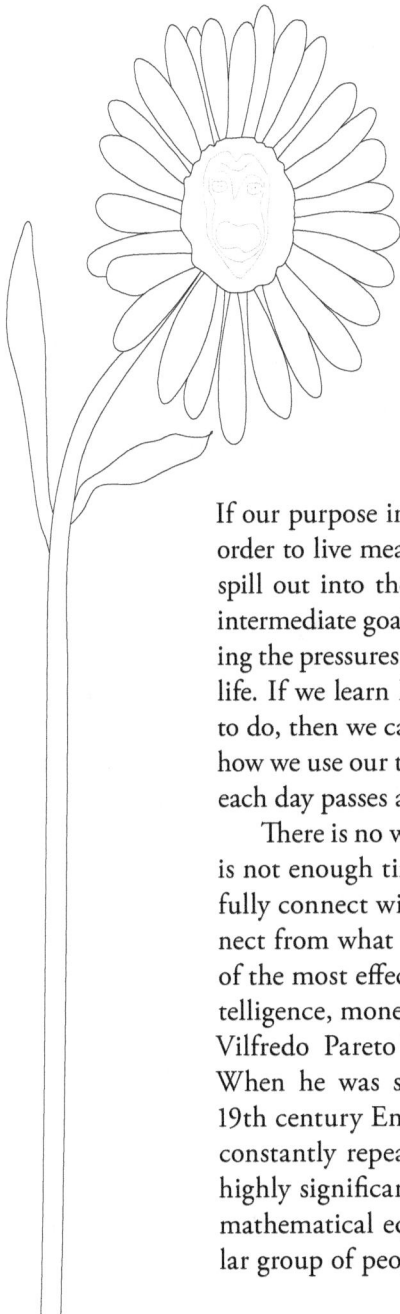

8

Disregarding the Irrelevant

Channeling Your Effort for Powerful Results

If our purpose in life is to use our strengths and talents in order to live meaningfully, be joyful, and allow that joy to spill out into the world in the service of others, then our intermediate goals must attend to the business of transcending the pressures, strains, overloads, and stresses of everyday life. If we learn how to make the most of what we choose to do, then we can use our time and energy effectively, and how we use our time and effort becomes more important as each day passes and our future opens in front of us.

There is no way we can participate in everything; there is not enough time. But how do we effectively and powerfully connect with what we want, and consciously disconnect from what we consider wasteful? In my opinion one of the most effective ways to manage our time, energy, intelligence, money, and effort is by using Pareto's principle. Vilfredo Pareto (1848–1923) was an Italian economist. When he was studying wealth and income patterns in 19th century England, he began to see patterns that were constantly repeated and he thought these patterns to be highly significant. One of these patterns was a consistent mathematical equation or relationship between a particular group of people and the level of income or wealth this group enjoyed. It is not surprising that a majority of wealth and most of the income went to a minority of people, but what was surprising was how predictable the relationship of this unbalance was.

Generally, these were his findings. If Pareto found 20% of the population held 80% of the wealth, then only 10% would enjoy 65% of the wealth, and merely 5% of the people would hold approximately 50% of the wealth. He found these patterns repeated themselves across populations in different areas. The point here is not the actual percentages, but how predictable the disproportion is in its repetition.

The 80/20 Rule

What became particularly exciting to Pareto was this predictable pattern of imbalance was also repeated when he looked at different time periods in England. When he looked further, he found this model again repeated itself in other countries and in their historical records, and still the relationships remained relatively the same. Here is where Pareto's imagination began to soar. He wondered if he looked at two related sets of data other than populations and wealth, would he see these same relationships?

The theory behind the 80/20 rule is that the minority of efforts, inputs, and causes will usually lead to the majority of rewards, outputs, and results. Just to say it very simply, 80% of the happiness you enjoy or the success you achieve in your life and your business comes from merely 20% of the time you spend pursuing it or the effort you spend achieving it. What does this mean for you? It is definitely scary, and it is understandable why most people do not want to look at this concept or admit it to be true. Does it mean four-fifths of your efforts are irrelevant? This is certainly counterintuitive to what we think, but some of your efforts may be just that, irrelevant.

In business environments it has been demonstrated that about 20% of customers account for about 80% of sales, and 80% of your revenue comes from 20% of your products. You already know from personal experience that you wear 20% of your clothes 80% of the time, and you spend 80% of your time in approximately 20% of your home. Consciously knowing this can be enormously powerful. With imagination, insight, and really looking honestly at what you do, how you do it, and when you do it, you can begin to harness and ignite the power held in the concept of imbalance. It is already coiled and waiting for you to use.

Five Ways to Maximize Your Assets

Everyone can be more fulfilled, content, and effective in their lives. Each of us can operate our businesses more profitably and with more efficiency.

Your self-awareness will help you identify your most productive actions; once you see them you will then ease into the appropriate substitutions. When you stop using or change the way you use resources that produce little benefit in one area, you can start using them only where they provide exceptional value. At the heart of this message is the idea that you can learn to live a better, happier, and more complete life through the art of substitution.

Your resources consist of five assets:

- Time
- Money
- Energy
- Intelligence
- Effort

By their intrinsic nature, these assets are limited and it is worth your best efforts to maximize their value. This is why identifying your talents and passions is so important to creating your life.

How we use one resource becomes how we treat another. I know when I become lazy and start frittering away my time, I do the same with my money, then my energy scatters, and my attention becomes unfocused. The effect can snowball, and when this happens assets will be wasted. It is when we weave and apply each of our five resources to our talents and passions that we truly come alive and become more powerful. When your assets, talents, and passions are integrated, you are living in alignment with yourself and your purpose; this is precisely when you will know that you are living a well-lived life.

Think about how great the waste is if 80% of the products, employees, and customers are producing only 20% of the profits. If 80% of your efforts are not building the peaceful, meaningful, and loving relationships you desire, this is a massive waste personally and globally. Does that mean you need to stop doing four-fifths of what you do right now? None of us want to admit we are this wasteful, and changing on that level is no small thing. Yet this amount of waste is staggering to the imagination. Once we see it, what else can we do? As you examine your life and decide to embrace change, think of what Theresa of Avila said, "Everything changes, only God is constant."

Living Your Life By Design Not Default

If you are interested in the idea of increasing personal productivity, universal happiness, and excellence, then shifting how and where you do things is absolutely necessary. Understanding and embracing all of your unbalanced activities allows you to make decisions that multiply everything of value. The actions you take can be simple. Consider moving an employee to an area where his or her contributions are more worthy and appreciated. Take your vacation in places that maximize what you value. Finally, learn to give to your loved ones in ways they value most; you will see the difference this makes in your relationships.

I believe that every single action and interaction have value and significance. Yet it cannot be ignored that a "vital few" of our actions have much more impact than the "trivial many." When these vital actions are identified and cultivated, their impact can be greatly expanded. Also if you are open, new applications can be found for once seemingly useless actions, which then could have the potential to create unbelievably valuable outcomes.

You could substitute a hobby for a lucrative small business. What do you do well, and what gives you satisfaction? If you have the ability to go into another person's home and rearrange the furniture to make the living space more beautiful and useful, then you could stage properties that are on the market for sale.

Social Inequity

At this point I want to make a few comments about cultural imbalance. Cultural inequity and the lack of hope it breeds, by its own definition, fails to use all human resources effectively. There are numerous personal, social, and spiritual reasons why inclusion is so important. Excluding people deprives them of developing their talents and deprives society of the benefits they could provide to the collective common good and the evolution of human consciousness.

One type of exclusion often overlooked is happening within today's community correction systems. In 2005 in the United States we had 5% of the world's population and 24% of the world's prisoners. That worked out to nearly 1 in every 115 Americans or nearly 3 million people living behind bars. In 2008 that number jumped to over 1 in 100 people in American prisons, the highest percentage, the highest number, and the highest per capita anywhere in the world. More than one percent of Americans are in prison and most of the crimes committed had nothing to do with violence. Even sentencing for petty theft can be the same as for grand larceny when we lose sight of a person's humanity and value, and begin to view him or her as unredeemable and unworthy.

It is obvious that there is a great waste of the prisoners' lives. But there are also millions of people involved in maintaining this large multi-layered system. What greater purpose does this serve in the evolution of human-kind? Without even looking at the billions of dollars spent by an entire industry built around exclusion, what real cost is paid by the public when a long-incarcerated person reenters society? Is this person ready, prepared, and openly accepted after completing his or her sentence? How could we possibly encourage, ignite and cultivate the five resources (time, money, energy, intelligence, effort) in others or ourselves, when we exclude people or purposely waste their valuable assets?

What does it say about a society that demonstrates waste on such a grand scale? On a personal scale, what kind of atmosphere do you create when you are with other people? Are you encouraging, do you look for faults? It is possible for us to create an environment where the world can come alive, but it will take effort and belief.

Imbalance Is Imperfect

Please keep in mind that the 80/20 rule is only a benchmark and the real numbers may be more or less unbalanced. The numbers do not have to add up to 100 because we are dealing with two distinct sets of data. Consider these examples. Merely 15% of the world's population uses 80% of the energy, 25% of the world's people hold 80% of the world's wealth, and in the United States less than 5% of the households own more than 75% of the entire American household equity. Since the 1980's fewer people have owned more every year. From these numbers, you can see these two percentages do not have to add up to 100. However, with these examples you get the idea about the comparisons. The 80/20 rule is imprecise, yet it can be understood as metaphor.

Even though imbalance is prevalent, it is not efficient, nor is it inevitable or desirable. Successful entrepreneurs focus on this predictable principle to make changes and maximize their profit-making skills. Consequently, this has been their secret: they find an imbalance, and then they focus their resources and unwaveringly apply them to make unproductive activities more productive. It is their insight, persistence, and consistency that make the difference; they put their effort into finding a productive use for every scarce and valuable resource. Successful entrepreneurs have learned to use the 80/20 rule to pursue progress and create an improved reality from their own initiative and vision.

There is always plenty of room for improvement. Just knowing this fact brings us great advantage; the problem is clear, improvement does not merely evolve on its own. Our ability to alter how we use our resources will begin with our desire and depend heavily on our ingenuity. Perhaps it could depend upon the level of your technology and your ability to build on past accomplishments.

When I took this knowledge and stood in front of my own closet, I knew it was a perfect example of Pareto's principle. Shoes, pants, tops, jackets, skirts, each category was imperfectly imbalanced. It was almost overwhelming. I thought, "How do I take control of this?" The answer lies in looking at each item individually, not at the whole. This not only applies to closets, it also applies to clutter that gathers in our homes and our behaviors. In fact starting with something concrete like your closet, desk, or kitchen can train your eye to critically analyze your behavior and what you accumulate in your life and let clutter your mind.

You begin by looking at each thing or thought individually, and then evaluating its usefulness. It becomes obvious the reason so much power is coiled within the 80/20 rule; the power is there because it is constant, predictably unbalanced, and counter-intuitive. In other words, you can count on this pattern or model to repeat itself over and over and over again. Because of this constant repetition we expect the imbalance, then we can examine it and exploit its potential. With this understanding, we can then leave behind the detrimental myth that all causes and effects are equal. When we honestly look at a situation, often the waste and imbalance is greater than we ever dreamed. The actual imbalance in your life is there for you to discover. Whatever it is, it is likely to be much greater than your estimate. Are you willing to look?

Reallocating Resources

The reallocation of resources always takes some type of initiation, a shove in the right direction. But what type of shove, and in what direction? Applying thoughtful, aware answers to these questions will make you money, increase your happiness, or build the standard of living and welfare of humankind. Finding your personal answers and direction will mean looking very closely at performances, but not performances and results as a whole. Generally, we average the effects of our efforts and judge the outcome on this aggregate. This does not allow us to see the importance of truly significant moments and actions, and meaningful experiences our efforts have produced.

You will need to slow things down to find the appropriate direction to take your business and life. When you simplify and carefully break down your actions and begin measuring the performance of your valuable resources individually and routinely, you will attain important and clear insights. By de-averaging the outcomes of your efforts, you will isolate the "vital few" powerful forces from your many actions which have weak or negative impact.

Then radical surgery is required. You have to take the intuitive path to reallocate your time, money, energy, intelligence, and effort, to where they are best used. This is the shove. Your solutions could be tiny or be far-reaching; however, they have one thing in common: they require your assets and resources to be used only where they are highly rewarded. By making the decision to decide in advance how to use your limited resources, you will reduce their squandering and increase your satisfaction and happiness. You can be retrained (and your employees can be retrained) to cut the waste, make what you do matter, and then be accountable for your actions.

Meaningful Disturbances

Making what you do matter is important for your well-being. There may be mundane everyday chores you consider unimportant, I urge you to look for meaning in them too. The more meaning you discover in everyday life, the lower your stress level, and conversely, the more decisive, content, and satisfied you become. This deepens your love for life and you find you want to be more accountable for what you do, because you are making the kind of difference you want to make. When what you do matters, you stop making excuses for yourself, your shortcomings, and the things you have not accomplished. When what you do matters, you learn from your mistakes and benefit greatly from your successes. In general, your life becomes authentically meaningful.

Generally everyone is reticent to make radical changes and simplify their lives and businesses. These changes disturb everything; we have become invested in our ideas and the way we have done things in the past, whether it is working and functioning for us or not. In reality, most people prefer the status quo and choose to remain unaccountable and unconscious. "We are on the verge of a whole new age, a whole new world. Human consciousness, our mutual awareness is going to take a quantum leap. As Paul Williams says, "Everything will change… All this is going to happen just as soon as you are ready."

Now that you know all of this, you can be among the few who live their lives consciously, see its fleeting preciousness, and maximize their meaningful moments. You can be the one who recognizes opportunities and chooses to live happily by your own design.

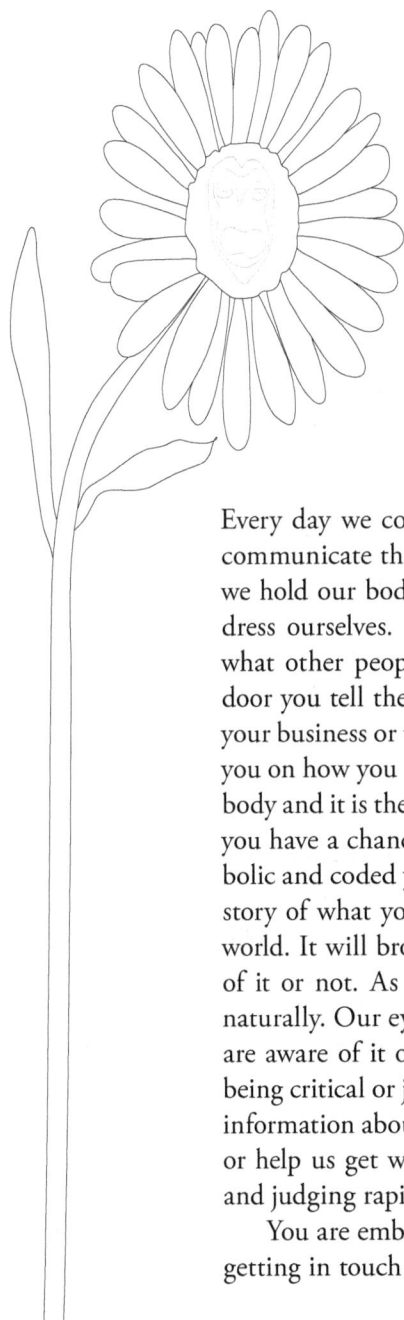

9

Presenting Yourself Well

The Messages of Clothing

Every day we communicate verbally and nonverbally. We communicate through facial expressions, gestures, the way we hold our body, the clothes we choose, and the way we dress ourselves. How you present to the world is exactly what other people see. Each day when you walk out the door you tell the world about you, you become the face of your business or the work that you do, and others will judge you on how you present yourself. Your clothing covers your body and it is the first to speak, and it speaks quickly, before you have a chance to. Clothing has its own language, symbolic and coded yet strong and loud. Your clothing tells the story of what you think of yourself and your place in the world. It will broadcast for you whether you are conscious of it or not. As humans, we tend to "read" other people naturally. Our eyes actively gather information whether we are aware of it or not. This may have nothing to do with being critical or judgmental. Often we are merely gathering information about our environment to assist in our survival or help us get what we want. Other times we are judging and judging rapidly.

You are embarking on a journey where you are actively getting in touch with what it means to be powerful. Power is subtle, yet very obvious. Personal power is reflected in your clothing, just like a mirror reflects you. Up to this point, you have been focusing on gathering the energy you have allowed to scatter. Now is the time to learn to be more aware of the messages you are sending and decide about their congruency. Then you can make conscious choices about how you want to be perceived.

Elements of nonverbal communications

Think back to how fast you have made assessments of other people; others are doing this to you too. Remember how it felt when you intuitively knew you were being judged? Next time as you meet a new client, speak with an unhappy customer, or interact with people at a party, consider the following elements.

- In face-to-face communication, nonverbal aspects form our first and greatest source of impressions.
- They are the measurement by which all your words and actions are judged.
- Then they structure all following interactions.
- They are more heavily considered if your look and words are contradictory.
- Finally, the nonverbal element is the most revealing difference between the powerful and the less powerful.

We are receiving and broadcasting information constantly, and a large component of this information comes in as visual clues. The most obvious and compelling visual indicators about you are your clothing and grooming. Your clothing's language projects your needs, personality, talents, and destination. Look at yourself in the mirror today and ask, "What is my destination?" Look closely, what conscious and unconscious thoughts and beliefs about yourself are you broadcasting?

The Value of First Impressions

If I am the first to tell you that within 10 seconds of entering a room, you have been completely evaluated by everyone who has glanced your way, at least you are hearing it now. I know, this makes my skin crawl, too. But I am not telling you this to make you anxious or send you running for cover; I mention it to help you become more aware and congruent in how you present yourself.

When people look your way, some have decided they want to get to know you better, others have totally written you off. After this incredibly short time, all subsequent information is used to back up his or her initial impression. Again, I am aware this sounds depressing; however, we do this every time we meet someone new. We are sleuths looking for evidence by using visual surface clues, and we quickly decide whether or not we have something in common with this fellow human being. Based on the person's clothing, hair, and demeanor we make snap judgments.

These quick appraisals are being made constantly, and they are that fast and that final. Once this judgment has been made, the content of your message will not change it. First impressions are lasting impressions. Whether you are engaged in a one-on-one interaction or walking to the dais for a presentation, if you have made a great first impression, you will hold your audience's attention. However if you have made a poor impression, you have lost them before you have started, no matter how compelling your message or worthwhile your ideas.

Negative imprints are very hard to overcome. It takes approximately seven positive encounters to overcome fixed objections made by a negative first impression. You may never get that many chances to recover. Imagine

---

Verbal versus nonverbal communications

Look at the following verbal and nonverbal communication components. Rarely are any of them ever used alone. Normally they are combined with one another and together they convey the overall impression you make.

Verbal	Nonverbal
Rate Of Speech	Facial Expressions
Choice Of Words	Posture
Tone Of Voice	Gestures
Attitude	Clothing
Enunciation	Hair
	Overall appearance

---

how much farther you could be in a relationship if you start out on the right foot with a good, even a great first impression.

Of course you want to be valued for who you really are—your deeper self, your capacity to love, your compassion, and your intelligence. Nonetheless, you may never get the chance if you do not connect from the beginning. How you act, look, and carry yourself is extremely important. Think about what you prefer, and how you have been attracted to someone in the past and then clicked instantly. On the other hand, there may have been someone whom you virtually disliked on sight, with whom later you became friends, but this is rare. We have all made judgments, and we have all had them made about us.

Dressing the Part

Assess what you want from your life or career. If you desire recognition, respect, or aim to make more money, dress as if you already have what you want. Maybe you have a plan that will save the planet and want an opportunity to present it. When you look polished, even when you dress casually, you'll be perceived as more astute and more professional.

Whether you are involved in business or you are at a social gathering, it is a plus to generate positive interest before you even say a word, just by the way you present yourself. Think of the investment you have already made in your education, career, building your business, and the time you have already devoted to developing who you are now. Do not waste time at this stage, time is one of your precious assets; once you give it away, you cannot get it back. Ask yourself, is it worth a few flattering well-cut outfits and additional pieces of clothing to complete your preparation?

Components of communication

As the saying goes, "you cannot, not communicate." Even what you withhold or do not say communicates something. What you wear, how you speak, and what you do or do not do, all communicate something. Look at the chart below: does it surprise you how we communicate with each other?

Words   7%

Tone (emotion, volume, pitch)   38%

Visual/physical aspects   55%

Contemporary dress codes have removed the protective wrapping of the business suit. As a result, your clothing now more than ever reveals your true nature. It begins to speak for you before your words ever have the chance. Does your clothing match your zeal for success or your zest for life? When you look successful, more success is attracted to you. Of course, once your pleasing image has opened the door for you, your personality, dedication, acquired skills, and the quality of your work will become most important. Give yourself a chance to succeed. Always look exceptional and you will have more opportunities for your skills to shine.

How We Convey a Message

It is possible you could be working way too hard to produce the effect you desire. If you are exclusively invested in the content of your message and ignore the power of your image, you are undermining your overall effectiveness. When considering your message as a whole, what you have to say is a very small part of communication. How you say it is even more important than your words.

As you can see in the box "Components of communication," your visual image, clothing, grooming, and posture constitute a whopping 55% of how other people are receiving any message you communicate.

It is not that we do not pay attention to our appearance; we do care tremendously about it and spend millions of dollars each year on it. The problem is that we spend so little attention on how our appearance affects other people and in return ourselves. From now on, be aware of your effect on others and use this knowledge wisely to give you an edge in communication, which you may have ignored in the past. Use what you have learned to allow your beautiful competent professional image to support you in each moment of every day.

Bringing Your Power Image Into Your Comfort Zone

Your image whether personal or professional is one of your fundamental success tools. A professional image is a power tool that gives you the ability to make things happen, perform your job well, and move you forward in your career. If you learn to consciously use your clothing and grooming as valuable social and business assets, they will ease you through any situation. Think about how you feel when you love your clothes and you know they are perfect for you and the occasion.

Look at the words below that spell out the concept and components of image. Each of these words can be a quick energy reference for you; used properly all of them are highly charged tools. If you pay attention to the power they hold, and implement the essence of their meaning into your comfort zone, they will give you an edge that will propel you to greater possibilities.

Impression

Movement

Attitude

Grooming

Etiquette

Each time you dress, dress to keep your power intact; preserve this as your underlying intention as you make all choices. You do not want to be overlooked when opportunities arise that can take you beyond your current level of success. These could be the very opportunities that would leap you beyond your present dreams. Create a powerful pulled-together image that is congruent with who you are now and the person you see in your vision. Make this image part of your life, and you will understand the power it contains.

Learning how to manipulate the image you project is not about being dishonest or pretending to be someone you are not. It is about getting in touch with your authentic self and encouraging new friends, clients, or co-workers to be receptive to the real you. When people are receptive to you, they can look beyond your packaging and pay attention to you and what you have to say and what you have to offer.

None of us want to look like a clone or a fashion robot. Expression of your individuality is very important. Expressed appropriately, individualism in your professional attire can engage significant magnetic attraction and activate unlimited possibilities. Yet, be aware that taking too many liberties with your self-expression can backfire (putting off some people), thereby limiting and restricting your prospects. Once you have limited yourself in the eyes of other people, it takes time to work yourself out of those confines. Does your self-expression attract success to you, or does it create a distraction making winning difficult?

Minimizing Visual Distractions

Visual distractions hold enormous negative power. They minimize your effectiveness by pulling attention off your message. When people are distracted, it is impossible for them to pay attention. They become confused about what you are saying, then your vision and message get lost in the distraction you have created, thereby diminishing their interest, and your personal power. When your personal power is diminished, the likelihood of your success is also diminished.

Other people cannot hear what you are saying when your physical appearance distracts or disturbs their focus. Distractions set up mental chatter, an invasive static so intrusive that it blocks communication. Listening with focus is difficult enough even among people who have each other's best interest in mind. With added interference our short human attention span is even shorter. Never underestimate distractions; they are powerful, formidable, and sometimes impossible to overcome.

Looking Believable

Not even your good grooming will cover up a lack of business and social skills, to succeed in your business or at any endeavor you must be competent, trustworthy, and credible. There is no shortcut to gaining expertise, you must put in the effort and do the work. But while you do, remember to always present an image that is congruent with your values and visually shows what is important to you. This presents a believable look, because looking believable puts people at ease and helps to create bonds and build trust with people.

Dressing to respect both yourself and your client means finding clothes that are in alignment with the true you, your skills, and goals; choose clothes that make you look competent and trustworthy. Looking believable is looking credible and accomplished in clothes that look natural on you. As you shop and choose new clothing, remember how important it is to be congruent and to avoid sending misleading and distracting messages.

Even if you have developed a habit of shopping impulsively, you are capable of making clothing choices that will keep your image congruent with your abilities. Let the language of your clothing communicate your message to the world. It will show the real you; there is no such thing as a neutral message. You are continually communicating something.

Combating Your Personal Saboteur

Are you consciously dressing casually to achieve success? Or are you unconsciously dressing down to sabotage your goals and dreams? If you are floundering in your career, are not achieving your goals, or lack a defined vision, you have a personal saboteur working behind the scenes. You can hear it talking to you when it tells you to "go ahead and wear that blouse, it's only a tiny stain, it's only a little tight, no one will notice if your shoes are dirty, wear them anyway, they're really comfortable, and it doesn't matter."

How you look does matter; it matters to how you feel about yourself and how others feel about you. When you know you could look better, you are uncomfortable. This creates a disruption in your normal bio-chemical functions and physically weakens you. Our minds and bodies are linked and one always affects the other. Think about it; remember when you have worn rumpled, torn, tired, or cheap garb, it engaged feelings in you that matched the clothing. To honestly live your vision, it is imperative that you are able to dress casually and still exude as much credibility, power, and authority as if you were wearing a traditional suit.

All of us battle our own personal saboteur from time to time. Your subconscious mind is very sensitive and powerful. It will magnify and expand whatever you internalize, including the way you think about yourself and the way you present yourself. If you wear shabby clothing you bombard yourself with negative images and thoughts. Negative imagery, self-talk, and doubt bleed off a tremendous amount of precious energy. None of us can ever afford to lose energy in that way; it is unnecessary. Stop the leakage, because energy is given to us in a limited supply until we learn how to use it wisely.

To keep your energy intact, be focused in the present time, on the job you are doing, on what you are able to effectively plan, and on what you are able to successfully accomplish in the moment. If you put your focus on presenting yourself well today, your vision for the future will be able to unfold naturally.

When you are not fully engaged in your life and allow your power to seep out, your thoughts spiral down, becoming more and more negative, creating self-talk like this: "I always wear the wrong thing, I'm invisible, I can't attract the client, no one will ever love me, I'm a loser." On the surface these thoughts may seem unimportant and have no enduring impact, but the fact is, negative thoughts have an insidious impact, and they weaken you. Always think well of yourself and dress thoughtfully, because if you continually meet clients or customers at the office or on the job site dressed like a slob, you are headed down a dismal career path.

What are you projecting by the way you dress? You will believe what you continually tell yourself; you will believe your own lie if you repeat it to yourself enough. Repetition has a lot of power, and a lie repeated over and over with conviction and emotion becomes believable, while the truth spoken in a calm and even tone can sound like a lie. You know this to be true because you have seen this happen over and over in life, when you watch the television news, or your politicians. If you have been lying to yourself by dressing down, this is something you can begin to change immediately.

Positive Personal Presentation

There is only one speck of the Universe you can control and that is you. Have you been doing your best? Does your overall personal presentation express respect for yourself, your family, workplace, clubs, career goals, business, clients, and overall professionalism? Be brave and take a quick assessment of yourself. Take a really good look at you.

Are you engaging your personal saboteur?

Answer the following questions honestly, and you will be able to use them as self-discovery.

- Are you comfortable with powerful people? Do you ever want to shrink or back away from well-dressed people? How do you feel about them? How do you feel about yourself?
- Have you ever had an unexpected meeting and felt you had to apologize for your clothing? Have you intentionally avoided a client because of your attire?
- When you catch a glimpse of yourself, do you cringe? Do you look like you think you look? Are your clothes neat? Are your shoes clean and brushed or polished?
- Do you think all your clothing has to be wash and wear? Do you feel because you own your own business, your dress standards can be more relaxed?

How did you feel when you read those questions? Did you get the kind of piercing gut reaction that makes you think about your behavior? Have you been crippling your chance for success because you present yourself too dressed down for conducting business? Just by being aware that you have sometimes been unconscious, you will initiate changes.

Changes are scary, but you can mitigate your fear by looking at it directly and seeing what it really is. Overcoming your fear will stop it from working against you and making you feel inept, it will change your habits and perspective and allow you to reach your true aspirations. Also, dressing appropriately brings people closer to you and helps build alliances and comfort. Even in small business, a take-me-seriously business image helps keep you from being a business fatality statistic.

Take control of what you can control; one of those things is the way you present yourself to the world. Being well-dressed opens doors for you; allow them to open. When you project a highly professional profile, you will be looking into a mirror that projects a vision of your future.

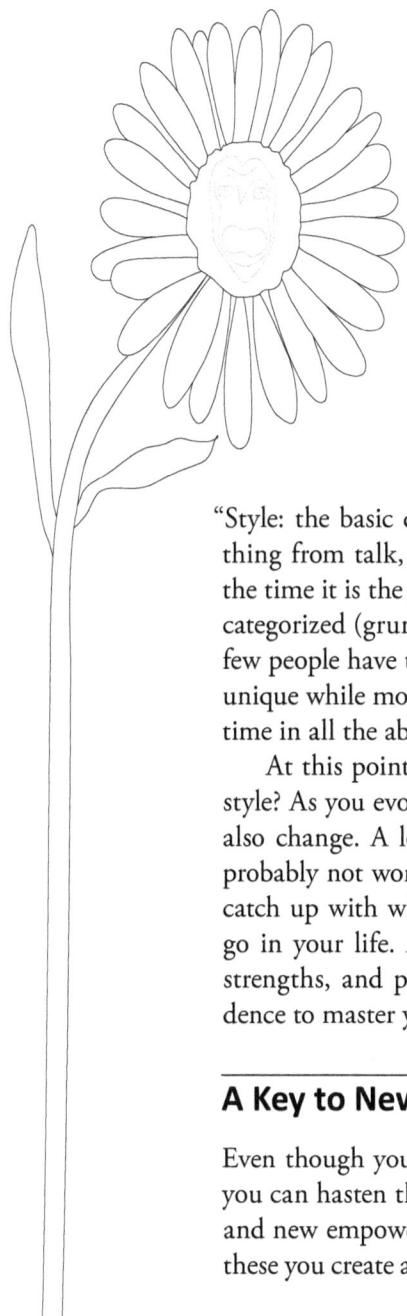

10
Dressing Up for Grownups
Find Your Style

"Style: the basic defining characteristics of a person, everything from talk, dress, hairstyle, demeanor. A majority of the time it is the person's appearance in general and can be categorized (grunge, hippie, preppy, hoochie, nerdy, etc). A few people have their own style which usually makes them unique while most go with whatever is the 'in' thing at the time in all the above categories." —Urban Dictionary

At this point you may be asking, what is my personal style? As you evolve and change, your style and image will also change. A look that worked for you in the past will probably not work for you today. Your image may need to catch up with who you are now and where you intend to go in your life. As you define your talents, identify your strengths, and put them to use, you will build the confidence to master your evolving personal style.

A Key to New Directions

Even though you cannot buy personal power, many times you can hasten the process of discovery with a new haircut and new empowering clothes that suit you perfectly. With these you create a shift in your perspective, allowing a closer connection to the true source of your power and vigor, the vibrating energy you have within you. This connection is enhanced and maintained when you dress thoughtfully, even when dressing casually.

As noted earlier in this book, people respond to the image you present to them. They will be comfortable with you in direct relation to how comfortable you are with yourself. Your attitude, confidence, and style are also reflected by the look in your eye and the expression on your face. What you believe about your abilities and yourself will be manifested in your style and visible for everyone to see. Your values determine how you approach life, and they in turn help form your attitude. Your style combined with your attitude can limit your possibilities or broaden them beyond your wildest dreams. Style can seem elusive yet it is attainable, valuable, and very important, because without style your great ideas may never be noticed and your ambitions misunderstood.

Connecting With Your Personal Style

It is natural to be reticent as you start the process of finding or developing your style identity. Knowing you do not have to spend a lot of money on a whole new wardrobe can ease your resistance to starting this process. Most likely your intuition has led you in the right direction already. Look at the "Seven Favorite Things" you listed in Chapter 2. How well have you integrated your style with what you value? This is the direction you will be taking your style development.

Begin by consciously looking at photographs in magazines. Look at fashion, pictures of places, and scenery, and choose swatches of fabric that appeal to you. Collect anything that attracts you and keep them in a folder. Let the collection happen naturally; try not to make judgments on the outcome. You will begin to see patterns emerge, color, shape, and a general mood of what you like. This knowledge about your style will help you evaluate the clothes in your closet and be your guide as you buy new pieces and outfits to complete your wardrobe.

Next, decide how you want the world to see you. You can write a clear concrete sentence or express this vision by using just a few words. Be sure to use descriptive words such as pretty, competent, and accessible or strong, kind, and smart. Keep working with the words you choose until you know they are right. When the words are clear and precise, they implant an image in your subconscious mind, which you will begin to fulfill. You will see the gap between reality and your vision, and your mind will naturally begin to work on bringing the two together.

Then you need to implement the actions to make your new and evolved personal style come alive. Gather all of your determination, go to your closet, and get rid of everything you own that undermines the essence of who you are and the image you intend to project. If you have not worn a piece of clothing or an outfit in a year or two, you probably do not like it that much. I am guessing you could be passing on 70%–85% of your wardrobe.

To keep a piece of clothing you should be able to answer yes to all of these questions:

- Do you love it, really love it? Just sort of liking it is not enough.
- Does it look magnificent on you? Honestly?
- You may love it, it may flatter you, but is this the image you want to project to the world?

Set a date to go through your closet if you have not done so already. This is one of the most important organizational actions you can do. If you do not love an outfit, if you do not look fantastic in it, or it undermines the image you want to create, get rid of it (of course, if you have some treasured piece to add to a fashion "archive," you can stow it away in a time capsule box to be looked at years down the road). Clothes can turn to clutter quickly, and clutter is distracting and takes up too much of your precious time and attention. You will get dressed a lot faster in the morning and it will be a huge relief when you do not have to work around all of the clothes in your closet that are not quite right.

Lastly, put any costumes, formal wear, or specialty items in the back of your closet or attic. You want them stored where they will not interfere or be in the way while you build your fabulous wardrobe and choose clothing that is a perfect fit for your new style. Remember, do not throw out costumes and formal wear; you will always need them for parties.

Before you hang your clothes back up in the closet, inspect each piece for repairs, examine hem and sleeve lengths, check all buttons, and then immediately arrange for the repairs to be made. Some repairs you will want to have done professionally; others you can quickly do yourself. Also check for fit; your body may have changed and look to see if you need to make any style alterations. It is always important for you to wear clothing that fits you perfectly, and at the same time feels great on your body.

Developing Your Style

Once you clear your closet—yes, this can take many weekends—begin to build your style by being sure of what you want for your life. Be patient, be definite and aim high, high meaning nothing less than what feels perfect for you. It is just as easy to aim high, to reach for the perfect style as for something less, and you will always have much better results. Your clothing can be a costume to make today more pleasurable and to create the future as you want it to be. When perfect it will convey your confidence and your willingness to reach out to others.

Reaching out to others is one of the most important things we ever do. This is how relationships are formed and power of connection is honed. Additionally, it is necessary to reach out to others, because we never create anything totally alone. Everything is built in alliance with the support and help of others, from the small to the very big important things in our lives.

There is great joy in living in clothes that fit you and fit your style perfectly. Besides, it's fun. Moreover, congruency, a state of harmony and agreement, is powerful and very attractive, and all of this is more easily conveyed when you combine it with comfort. Always be comfortable, because you live in the physical world, a place that requires your physical effort.

What About Comfort?

You can dress comfortably while suiting your personality, the job you want, or the work you are doing that particular day. It is necessary to be comfortable, because comfort is essential to an authentic professional or social image. Yet comfort must come from quality fabrics and proper fit, not simply throwing on sloppy loungewear. Just because the job you are doing may require physical labor, you need not dress like a slob. When you dress carelessly, everyone around you including your clients cannot easily envision your competence and you performing well for them. This is very often the bottom line to people: They ask themselves, "How will your performance affect me, how will you make me look?" Ask yourself, "When I meet people, will I deliver a positive or negative impression?"

In business as well as your personal life it is very attractive when you are authentic, honest, and sincere. All of that is already a part of who you are. Sometimes you merely need to become more in touch with those qualities. This is a whole lot easier to accomplish when you are comfortable in your clothing. Remember, you can add to the impact by using your beautiful smile and open body language to project confidence, believability, and trustworthiness. Practice the body language of confidence and it will adopt you.

Invest in Quality

Do you know what other signals you are sending? Success leaves clear visual clues in your appearance, and those clues speak clearly to you and to all the other people with whom you interact. What is the condition of your clothing and the quality of its fabric? It's not only your clothes; your shoes, hair, nails, and jewelry all send visual clues about your personality, what you believe about yourself, and your level of success.

Never underestimate the value of quality because it is definitely noticed. Looking for quality does not mean being a slave to name brands or designers. I can walk through a thrift store touching a rack of $10 pants and find the finely woven Italian wool. With a little practice you too can become an expert at finding great fabrics, construction, and fit that works for you. Touch the fabrics, use your creativity, and try different styles as you continue to create your well-coordinated look.

Take the time to learn what quality looks and feels like. This is an important investment; when you invest in yourself, you will find the world is willing to invest in you also. It all starts with taking care of yourself, so love yourself enough to make the dramatic changes inside and out which are necessary to reach your vision and get everything you want out of your life. Once you are filled up, you can then take care of the world.

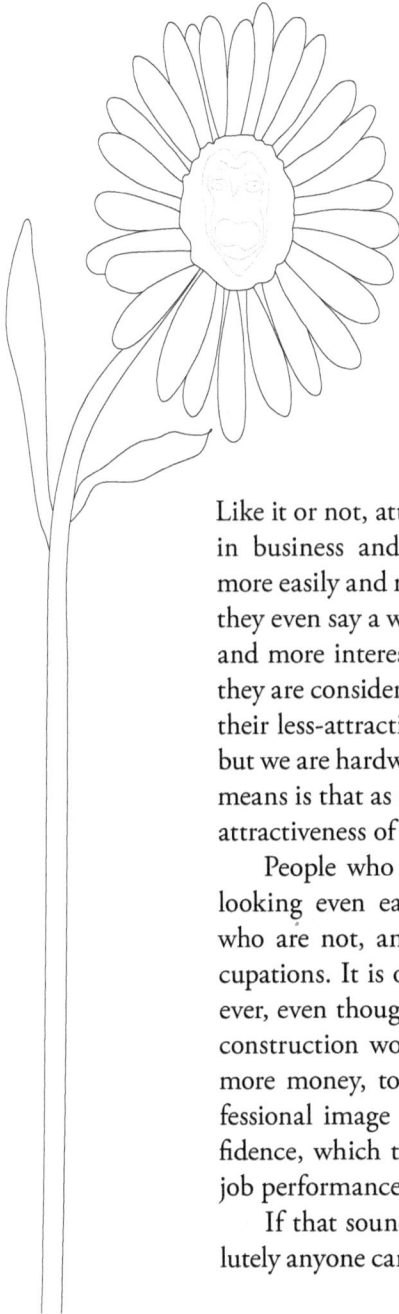

11

Tapping Into Attraction

How to Be More Magnetic

Like it or not, attractive people have tremendous advantage in business and social interactions. Everything happens more easily and more smoothly for attractive people. Before they even say a word, they are perceived to be more likeable and more interesting. Before they even present their ideas, they are considered more intelligent and more credible than their less-attractive colleagues. I know this sounds shallow, but we are hardwired for survival, and one of the things this means is that as a species we have evolved to respond to the attractiveness of other people.

People who are perceived as being attractive or good-looking even earn considerably more money than those who are not, and this phenomenon reaches across all occupations. It is obvious that good looks help in sales; however, even though this seems incredible, similarly endowed construction workers and telemarketers make about 20% more money, too. I feel this is because an attractive professional image fosters higher self-esteem and greater confidence, which then translates into better focus and better job performance.

If that sounds depressing, here is the good news: absolutely anyone can be perceived as attractive. To be perceived as attractive, you do not have to be movie star handsome or breathtakingly gorgeous; it comes from knowing your qualities. Also, when the 20% salary advantage is more closely examined you will find most of the difference is found between the categories of perceived homely and good-looking. The premium for beauty is only 3%, and I believe "perceived homely" merely means "given up."

As you develop your style, ask others for feedback and keep track of what they say about your best features. Most people are not in touch with their most appealing qualities and therefore have no idea how to maximize their attractiveness. Put in the effort and do your research to make the most of what you have, because as you magnify your qualities, you will magnetize yourself. It will be worth your time and effort.

Tuning In to Five Attractive Qualities

Being attractive is not elusive; it is within your reach. When you practice these five qualities, people will be attracted to you.

These qualities are the secrets to vanquishing loneliness and the keys to developing relationships with other people:

- ⮞ Carrying yourself well
- ⮞ Exuding confidence
- ⮞ Having a sincere smile
- ⮞ Maintaining a positive attitude
- ⮞ Exhibiting genuine joy

When you meet other people with a smile and receptive attitude rather than critical judgment, you will discover that you are more likely to find out who they truly are, and they will be interested in finding out more about you.

Conversely, if these qualities are not activated, you could spend an evening at a party or a week at a convention and never meet any one. When you focus on what is wrong with everyone, you bring yourself loneliness, no one discovers your fine qualities, and you know nothing about theirs. Think what a waste of our human resources that represents. But if you are open and accepting, it will put magic in your life. Anthony Robbins put it this way, "If we believe in magic, we will live a magical life. If we believe our life is defined by narrow limits, we've suddenly made those beliefs real." Expand your limits by combining these five attraction qualities with flattering clothes, well-done makeup, and excellent grooming, you definitely will be perceived as striking and stunningly attractive.

Have you activated your attractive qualities?

In your own experience, remember how you have noticed people you thought were attractive. Attractive people get noticed. To become aware of how you now think about attraction, go through the following exercise.

1. People have attempted to step in front of you in line.   Yes=-1, No=+1

2. You often receive compliments from people in positions of power.   Yes=+1, No=-1

3. You have to ask for a good table in a restaurant. Yes=-1, No=+1

4. You readily attract the type of person you want to do business with.   Yes=+1, No=-1

5. You readily attract the type of person you want as a friend or lover.   Yes=+1, No=-1

6. Strangers smile at you.   Yes=+1, No=-1

7. You have enough money to be satisfied and be comfortable.   Yes=+1, No=-1

8. People usually listen attentively when you speak. Yes=+1, No=-1

9. You have been passed over for promotion or didn't get a job you wanted.   Yes=-1, No=+1

Rate Your Attraction Quality

0-3 You are in danger of being invisible to yourself and others. Often your goals seem unattainable. You seriously need more self-esteem and a perception change.

4-5 You need a boost of self-esteem and confidence and are sometimes susceptible to the hurtful comments and acts of others. Start today to consistently believe in yourself.

6-7 You are on your way, you know how to treat yourself, but do not always follow through with your good intentions.

8-9 You've made it, you love high-quality everything, you know how to live and present yourself, and you do it.

Take the quiz on the previous page, and look at the results. What did you learn? Do you need to activate more attraction? If you start to make the most of your assets by playing up your most appealing qualities, you will begin to attract more of everything. As you allow yourself to evolve and become closer to your ideal, you will energetically move closer to what you want to attract. At that point you will begin to attract the people and business into your life you really want. It is natural for people to be attracted to others similar to themselves. This is exactly what it means to engage the law of magnetic attraction. It is activated either positively or negatively. If you choose to be cruel and manipulative, that is what you will see in the world, and that is exactly what you will attract.

If you must engage with people who live and work in toxic environments, how you react to them will have significant impact on your life. Do not choose to be drawn into the negativity, it will undermine your power and happiness. My advice is to simply separate yourself or limit the time you are willing to spend with people who live dishonestly or "live to create drama" in the world. Live with your own truth and your own standard of honesty and you will draw to you what you need and want most. Continually support yourself by using the things you have learned about activating your attractiveness. Attractiveness creates appeal, and appeal is personally and professionally empowering.

Using Feedback as Intelligence

None of us want to be ruled by other people's judgments or fall into excessive pleasing behavior. We take pride in living our own lives and making our own choices. Yet we do not live in a vacuum, we live in communities and it is within this context that we make and measure all of our choices. Once we make a decision, we use other people's responses to guide us to our goal. Their responses let us know if we are on the right track or way off course, and these are important clues to our survival and drawing to us what we want in our lives.

When we receive this feedback, it comes to us in both positive and negative forms. It can be extremely difficult to stay conscious through receiving negative feedback. When people give us negative feedback, our immediate response is to lash out, label them as complainers and difficult, then disregard anything they have to say.

Maybe it is true, they are negative and toxic, but it may also be that you can benefit from what they have to say. Try to accept both styles of feedback as a gift. Be thankful for everything you hear, and then solicit more information even though it may also be painful to hear. Sometimes the negative feedback is way more important to you than any compliment you could ever receive. If you can be open-minded, neutral, and pay attention to what is said, then you can react accordingly and gain significantly. Of course this is very difficult to navigate; however, it is not impossible.

Projecting Your Best Assets

Always be very aware of how other people perceive you. What are you truly projecting? Becoming conscious of other people's responses to you takes paying close attention to their reactions. Your image may be conveying something completely different than you intend. You may think you are projecting a casual image that says, "I'm successful, I don't have to work for someone else," when in fact your client may see someone who lacks success, ambition, and professionalism. Learn to evaluate the tiny nuances of how others respond to you, because then, you will know if you are on the right track to building more meaningful closer relationships or attaining a successful career.

When you are impeccably well-dressed you feel magnificent, confident and powerful, your generosity is expansive, and your self-esteem rises. You can then afford to be magnanimous, complimentary and attentive to other people. As you lift out of yourself and reach for more, you will become more open in the world and your environment becomes more accessible, brighter, and beautiful. As you give more, your world expands, and what you receive in return can never be predicted. All of this combines to build your energy and provide the confidence to take risks and achieve in a world that reflects your own outlook.

Self-Awareness Has Rewards

Now that you know you are constantly sending signals to other people and that every communication affects the way others respond to you, you can use this information to shape your silent signs and messages to be in alignment with your true self. Signals are the physical embodiment of communication and their congruency with your essence is very attractive. Once you become aware of their presence you can let your signals work for you, and you can learn to let them integrate silently and naturally through your movements and your work.

All of the messages you receive, along with your interpretation of them, go to your unconscious mind and affect the attitude you have about yourself. Then subconsciously and insidiously the attitudes you form affect your demeanor. It is within your body that you carry your deepest truths about yourself. You have seen the weight of the world on a friend and have felt it for yourself. Conversely at other times, you have felt lifted and light, almost as if you were floating through the world barely touching the surface of the Earth.

Your demeanor reflects your deepest beliefs about yourself. It affects the way you carry yourself and hold your body. Your thoughts are revealed in the way you walk, talk, breathe, and behave in general. Your demeanor is a mirror to your soul and reveals your hopes and fears, and what you think you will able to receive in your life. Your demeanor is obvious to everyone and affects how other people will respond to you.

Positively or negatively, this becomes a cycle that reinforces itself, yet when you become aware of this pattern, your demeanor becomes something you control. This is the reason it is so important to accentuate the positive. Not false and meaningless affirmations, or being blind to your shortcomings; just acknowledge them and then focus what you can grow, your attractiveness and your power. Your mother knew a universal truth when she told you to sit or stand up straight. As you can see, being truly self-aware, using your strengths, and playing up your assets will build and maintain a powerful presence and an empowering image.

Becoming Fluent in Attractiveness

Critics are amazingly adept at identifying even the most-minute weakness. They are practiced experts and can home-in skillfully, make the attack, and back out unnoticed, leaving a lot of damage. Clever critics recognize insecurities hovering around your shortcomings. My advice is to diffuse the critic and simply accept your weaknesses while you accentuate your positive assets; this will grow your confidence and increase your attractiveness.

You are always conveying and reading nonverbal messages, they never shut down, and you never stop noticing. When you learn to listen and observe the language of nonverbal communication, you can become fluent in its reading and understanding. Empowering images always send signals both ways, they go to other people and to your own subconscious mind. It is within your ability to have this silent language work for you. Each day make a habit of being extremely kind to yourself, inside and out. Your kind habits will build a wonderful life today, and pave the path of your future.

The law of attraction is a universal truth; it manifests itself across all cultures in all languages, only its form differs. It is alive in bacteria, insects, and right up through primates. Attraction is the underlying principle behind the saying, "birds of a feather flock together." This truth is powerful and you can consciously harness its rewards.

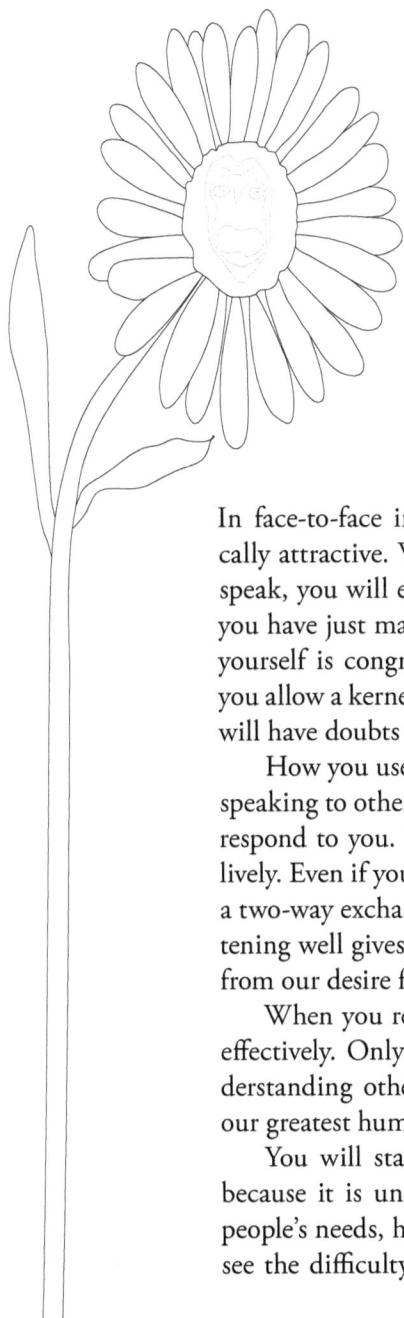

12
Powerful Speaking
For Understanding,
Introspection, and Compassion

In face-to-face interactions, it is not enough to be physically attractive. When you open your mouth and begin to speak, you will either confirm or deny the first impression you have just made. Even if the way you dress and present yourself is congruent with your abilities and strengths, if you allow a kernel of doubt to enter your voice, your listener will have doubts too.

How you use your voice creates a climate when you are speaking to other people, and it precipitates how others will respond to you. The atmosphere can be thick or it can be lively. Even if you are in front of a group, communicating is a two-way exchange and speaking is only one part of it. Listening well gives us an understanding of other people, and from our desire for understanding flows respect for all life.

When you respect others you can speak to them more effectively. Only one person in 10,000 is interested in understanding other people, yet being understood is one of our greatest human needs.

You will stand out if you seek to understand others, because it is uncommon. If we do not understand other people's needs, how could we possibly meet them? You can see the difficulty involved in being understood. Yet to be successful you must be understood, and therefore it is imperative you learn to express yourself effectively.

Being Understood

When you speak you reveal your personality and attitude. If your voice sounds harsh and abrasive, you will most likely be viewed as harsh and abrasive. If your voice sounds timid and insecure, you will most likely be considered timid and insecure. Conversely, if you sound confident and powerful, then chances are you will be thought of as a confident and powerful person. If your voice does not convey your energetic qualities, it is possible to train your voice to project your strengths.

As you understand more about your voice and how to control it, the more powerful your voice can be. Our voices not only have emotional impact, they affect our listeners physically, which is one reason we are so sensitive to the tiny variations and nuances of sound. These physical responses are part of our inherited human evolution and have been integral to the survival of our species as we have developed, and they are still vital today.

Even the anticipation of being spoken to abrasively evokes a physiological response in me. If I took my blood pressure before I went to a certain office in my community, I am sure it would be elevated.

Take a moment to examine the physical responses below and then test them on yourself and others:

- ᴥ Speak at a rapid rate and your listener's heartbeat rises, the adrenaline flows, and the breathing may become shallow.

- ᴥ Shout and it may cause your listener's blood pressure to rise.

- ᴥ Speak slowly and quietly and your listener reacts by becoming sleepy.

Creating More Power in Your Voice

Your voice is an essential tool for reducing tension and anxiety, and conveying control. It is possible to moderate your own voice so that you reduce your level of stress. Your voice is so versatile that when necessary it can also energize situations and stimulate activity. The sound of your voice can even relieve your own fatigue. Your voice is so subtly powerful it not only has direct physiological effects, it is also finely tuned to effectively broadcast both your physical and emotional states to people with whom you are speaking.

Vocal Indicators

Your voice can reveal your stress level before any other physical signs show. It reveals your level of fatigue, your energy, and your emotional state. If you listen you can hear reticence or excitement, sadness or joy; the entire spectrum of emotions can be heard through the human voice.

When you learn to tune into other people's voices, you will tune into their feelings, which are not easily masked vocally. Think of how many times you have been speaking with friends and clients on the telephone when you detect subtle changes in their voice. Those minute, subtle changes registered strongly on your conscious mind. Whether or not they initiated a response from you was a decision you made. Periods of silence and sighs sometimes speak as loudly as any spoken word.

To increase your knowledge of vocal sounds, use your own voice as a model for analysis and improvement. Get to know your voice and how it sounds in different situations. What changes do you notice in your voice when you are with different people? Do you initiate the changes or do they happen spontaneously?

Become aware of how your voice sounds, once you do you will know where and how to make improvements and learn to speak confidently and powerfully. Begin by recording three samples of your voice, for a duration of three minutes at different times of the day:

- **First** thing in the morning, record your voice when you are relaxed and fresh.

- **Next**, record your voice in the afternoon when your stress and exhaustion are at their highest.

- **Last**, record it in the evening when you are relaxed, but tired.

You can record a conversation or read a letter aloud, or possibly tell a story, or recite a favorite poem. Listen to these recordings to understand the importance of breathing and to learn to hear the vocal characteristics of rate, loudness, and pitch along with quality and articulation.

What did you learn by listening to your voice? How does your voice compare to your vocal role models? What have others said about your voice? I suggest you get feedback from everyone you can, your friends, colleagues, and professionals. If necessary, you may want to enlist the help of speech therapists and voice coaches. Learning how your voice sounds to others is the most important key to improvement. Just knowing that you need to add more power or softness to your voice allows you to adjust those qualities. Every voice can be improved if its owner is committed to working on it. Since you already spend much of each day speaking on the phone and in person, this means you will have lots of opportunity for practice.

Presenting Your Ideas Effectively

To convey your ideas effectively, use powerful language. Organize your ideas, and choose appropriate evidence to support them. How you organize and support your ideas adds to the effectiveness of the impression you make. You can have a beautifully trained voice, and if your facts are outrageous and unsubstantiated, you will create verbal distraction.

Powerful Language

Powerful language attracts others to you in much the same way as a powerful voice and powerful body language. It is not necessary to use big, obscure, and multi-syllable words for your language to be powerful. Clear concise words that express your ideas effectively are far better.

Sometimes it is about what you take out of your language that makes the greater difference. Excessive slang can be very distracting, yet well-placed slang words are expressive. A small amount of self-deprecation shows you encounter the same trouble and problems others face. But if you use it too much, other people will doubt your abilities and knowledge.

Organized Presentation of Ideas

When people get past what they see in your appearance and how your voice sounds, they are more receptive to hearing what you have to say. They are ready for the 7% of communication your words have to contribute, so organize them clearly. Even if you are intelligent, if you are vague and unclear in your presentation, you will not be seen as smart. How well are you able to convey your expertise? Experience and knowledge do not lie in your outward appearance even if you look great; you must articulate your ideas in a way others can and want to understand.

If you do not present your ideas in a manner the other person perceives as coherent and orderly, you may give the impression you are ill prepared, disorganized, and scatterbrained. Here is an example of how this can happen. My friend Jim Parker is one of the premier balloon drop engineers in the world. Balloon drops are timed performances at major events. Often when he was in a venue presenting a proposal to a client, he would begin to look at the ceiling to check the availability of rigging points.

Even with his expertise, can you believe this man who basically wrote the book on balloon drops, would sometimes not be hired to implement a drop in a venue? Why was this? Because the client, who was worried about how she would look to others, thought Jim was not focused on her or her event. Jim admits this happened more than once.

Now Jim arrives early to examine the venue to discern his options, and he makes sure he knows what the client is thinking and wants; then he shares his ideas, looking directly at the person. He organizes his presentation and chooses his words to integrate both points of view, and intentionally keeps his focus on the client. I know this story because my friend observed his own behavior, became aware of the fault, learned from it, and shared his experiences with others.

Appreciation of Learning Styles

People are not only diverse in appearance; they organize their thoughts and learn about the world differently, too. These differences are based on many factors, including our culture, education, and even on how our brains process information. Simplistically, some of us are inductive; we move quickly from specific information to a general conclusion. Some of us are deductive; we begin with a general concept and then we fill in the details. If you pay attention, with some practice you can adjust your style of delivery to match how your listener processes information.

Even among the inductive and deductive learning styles, we learn differently. Some of us learn more easily by hearing, others by seeing what is around them. Other people want to touch and manipulate the world in order to learn about it. When you know people listen and learn differently, you can vary your descriptive language so it is more easily understood by many people. Your words can paint a picture that describes a situation, an object, human emotion, or even the evolution of an untouchable concept.

At different times during our human life we want different things. Sometimes building community is the most important thing to us, other times we are looking for self-actualization. We may want to save the planet, or the search for meaning has captured our focus. As we grow and mature, our thinking passes through many levels and changes. Speak to these differences, too.

It is important for you to organize your thoughts and examine your patterns of thinking so that your ideas appear clear and orderly. If they are well thought-out and concisely presented, you will be listened to. However, remember never to underestimate your listeners' intelligence or overestimate their desire or need for information.

Four Steps to Speaking Easily

- **First**, find common ground right away by listening deeply. Consciously look for a reason to speak to the person engaging your attention.

- **Next**, explore and discover the other person's needs and desires by asking pertinent questions and listening to the answers.

     ~ **Then**, match those needs and wants with the best you have to offer. In business this may mean repackaging what you have—your expertise, product, or service—to appeal to the other person and to current evolving styles. In social situations it may simply mean making the other person feel comfortable.

     ~ **Last**, consciously clear away all of the obstacles and roadblocks you have created for yourself. It is then that you can start to communicate easily in a clear atmosphere.

People listen with their ears, but they listen from their hearts, too. Learn to speak from your heart, and you will give people a reason to listen to you speak.

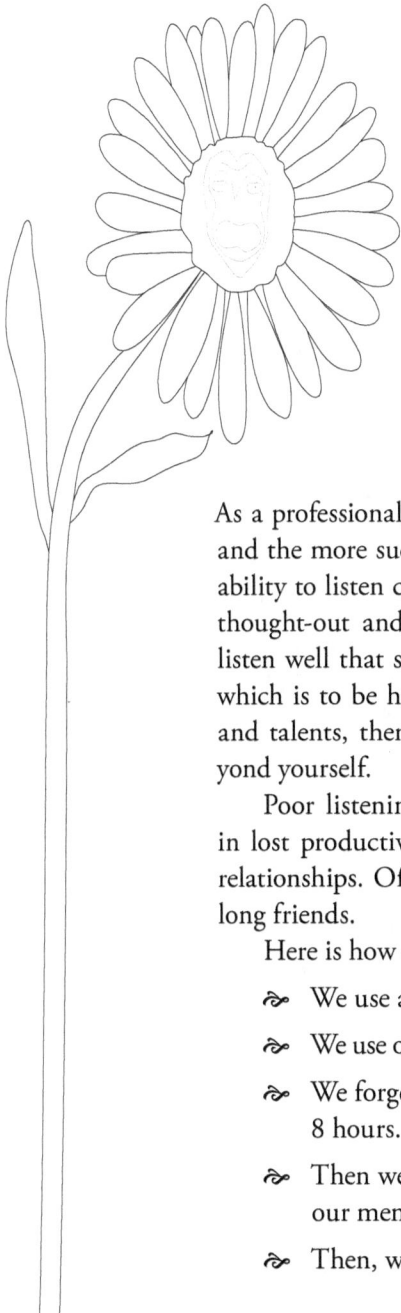

13
Powerful Listening
The Art of Building Meaningful Relationships

As a professional, most of your day will be spent listening and the more successful you are the more you listen. Your ability to listen closely gives you the capacity to make well-thought-out and intuitive decisions. It is your ability to listen well that supports you to pursue your life's purpose, which is to be happy, to get in touch with your strengths and talents, then use them successfully for something beyond yourself.

Poor listening habits cost us tremendously each year in lost productivity as well as losses in our interpersonal relationships. Often we do not even listen well to our life-long friends.

Here is how our listening skills tend to be applied:

- ❧ We use about 25% of our listening capacity.

- ❧ We use only about 10% of our memory potential.

- ❧ We forget 50% of what we're heard within 8 hours.

- ❧ Then we forget 90% of what we have heard, if our memories are not cued by something later.

- ❧ Then, we distort what little we do remember.

As you can see, these limitations leave very little room for deep and accurate listening in our communication, when we listen unconsciously. This is why it is unusual and outstanding when someone does listen. One of the rarest gifts ever given is the gift of being listened to. What excuses and explanations for poor listening do we tell others and ourselves?

Following are some of the reasons I have heard, and I am sure you could add others to the list.

- ❧ Humans have an attention span of less than 45 seconds; after that our minds wander.

- ❧ We are not formally taught to listen.

- ❧ We think 3–4 times faster than we talk.

- ❧ We filter everything others say through our own mental screen; for that reason it is difficult to avoid distortion or bias.

Have you felt yourself engaging in bad listening habits and then making excuses for your behavior? Becoming a better listener can begin immediately and you will notice the benefits immediately also. When people meet you for the first time, what kind of listener are you? What sort of impression do you send by the way you listen? Poor listening can show a lack of interest and conveys boredom, indifference, even hostility. Is that really the message you want to send?

Fortunately, listening, just like other skills, can be improved if you want to be a better listener. With effort, attention, and practice listening becomes easier because you want to focus on what people are saying and you want to fully understand them. If you adhere to the following sequence, you will get powerful results:

- ❧ **First**, you must be open to the idea and willing to improve your listening ability. Knowing that you need to improve your listening is the motivation that will get you started.

- ❧ **Next**, you need to have a sense of how you listen.

- ❧ **Last**, you need specific techniques to practice as you steadily and continually raise the quality of your listening skills.

How Attentively Do You Listen?

Good listening has the power to create sparks in a relationship. It will attract people to you, draw them closer, and make them feel understood and valued. Your clothes, tone of voice, and your powerful language cannot keep the interest of others if you continue to listen poorly and appear to be bored. People have interesting stories to tell and there is much to be learned from each person's life if you have the desire to listen. Truthfully answer "Eight Revealing Questions." Notice where you were right about yourself, and notice what inconsistencies you see in your behavior.

If you said yes to even one of the eight questions below, you know there is room for improvement. Pause now. Think of the times you have been the recipient of poor listening. They are easy to remember: the bored hotel clerk, the impatient teacher, the hostile or indifferent sales associate—the list goes on and on. These experiences are a continual source of irritation and frustration for everyone.

Eight revealing questions

Given what you have learned about listening so far, what do you think about yourself as a listener? Do you have a sense of how attentive a listener you are?

- ⮞ Are you easily distracted or bored, especially if you perceive the other person to be of lower status, less powerful, or not very attractive?
- ⮞ Do you listen with the attempt to evaluate, listening for facts, regardless of the type of message the person is trying to convey?
- ⮞ Do you withhold feedback, or show a lack of response by not looking at the talker or by maintaining a blank look on your face?
- ⮞ Do you normally interrupt others or feel impatient with how and what they are saying?
- ⮞ Do you focus on others' appearance or how they deliver the information, to the exclusion of their ideas and the content of their message?
- ⮞ Do you focus on the content of the speaker's message and ignore the subtle vocal and nonvocal delivery cues?
- ⮞ Do you let the emotion of the language disturb, distract, or excite you?
- ⮞ Do you listen with only part of your attention, because you are already planning your rebuttal?

Poor listening is a perpetual impediment when we are merely trying to convey a message or request information. Imagine how this is amplified when you have intricate or meaningful thoughts to communicate.

How to Spot a Poor Listener

Poor listeners show distinct patterns in their body, use of language, and tone of voice. These patterns are consistently repeated, and we pick up on them both consciously and subconsciously. This is typical of what happens. If they start out with eye contact, poor listeners will then usually look over your shoulder or to the side as if looking for someone or something more interesting. Their face may be blank or they will have a scowl pasted on it and their eyes might check their watch or a clock on the wall. What you will not see is a genuine smile, the kind of smile that reaches their entire face and shines through their eyes.

When you check out the rest of the poor listener's body language, it is just as closed off. Their shoulders are even more revealing; they are probably turned slightly away from you and their hands may be placed on their hips or in their pockets. Look at their arms and you could see them crossed like a roadblock across their chest. Poor listeners will often pick imaginary lint off their clothing, tap their fingers, and fidget. In general what you will not see is the open and involved body language that makes you feel heard and accepted.

Next listen to the poor listener's voice. You will hear phases and sounds like, I see, uh-huh, and hmmm, and not much else. They will interrupt with the intention to move you forward and hurry you along. And when they do speak to you, you will wonder if the two of you were having the same conversation. Notice how the poor listener will latch onto or challenge an obscure detail within the conversation that had little to do with your message.

Also listen for clichés that do not truly fit what has been said. Or maybe they will launch right into a story of their own using the dubious segue, "that reminds me," thus effectively ending a two-way dialogue. I am sure these descriptions evoke memories of past conversations that were not altogether pleasant. What was your position during the interaction? Normally each of us has seen both sides.

Are You Listened To?

Why are some people listened to and others are not? Answering this question will give you insight into why you have not been listened to, and conversely why you have sometimes stopped listening. There is a direct correlation between perceived authority and listening attentiveness. People do not listen well to other people whom they consider unattractive, not very credible, or inferior to themselves.

Even people who consider themselves to be kind and compassionate make excuses and judgments when they listen poorly, and then they defend themselves. Doing this is also part of what it means to be human. Yet, when you make judgments, you cut yourself off, scatter your energy, and weaken yourself. We have all done it, but we can unlearn it.

If you go into a conversation with any of these attitudes, you are not listening. You can make excuses, but the bottom line is that you are not listening. You are blocking yourself from meaningful interactions and it is absolutely certain you are going to miss important details and information.

In business, missing information could cost you tremendously in lost production because of misunderstandings. Appointments have to be rescheduled, orders are shipped wrong, late, or not at all. When people have to repeat themselves, they become uncomfortable, and when customers have to repeat themselves, they become irritated or furious.

Building Trust and Personal Bonds

Listening deeply builds trust and personal bonds with everyone, including your family, friends, and clients. Besides taking less time and being more efficient than poor listening, the interaction is more accurate with the first exchange, building confidence and understanding between people. Both

---

Reason for not listening

Do you recognize the following statements and excuses as ones you've heard or used to defend yourself for not listening well?

- ❧ They say the same thing every time.
- ❧ They have nothing to say that I don't already know.
- ❧ They waste my time.
- ❧ They just want to hear themselves talk.
- ❧ They are just interested in their own problems and nothing else.
- ❧ They don't look me in the eye.
- ❧ They bore me.
- ❧ They are always complaining.

---

people feel better about their interaction, which then encourages deeper relationship bonds. Imagine the possibilities that can open to you when you build relationships based on understanding and trust.

You do not have to agree with someone to listen to what they are saying, and you do not have to like someone to agree with what they are saying. When you truly listen you open yourself to a bigger world. Then when it is time for you to talk, you will have more to say because you listened with interest to many people and discussed many diverse subjects.

Three Basic Listening Skills

- ➤ Practice adapting your style of listening to fit the situation and the context of the message.

- ➤ Make an attempt to reduce interpersonal, cultural and environmental barriers that could hinder communication.

- ➤ Listen actively, and give feedback both verbally and nonverbally.

Expanding Your Listening Style

Mastering basic listening skills is not difficult; however, it does take willingness, insight, self-assessment, and a basic understanding of your current listening habits. Before you start this process, you need to pay attention to what is happening around you:

- ➤ **First**, eliminate or minimize all of the distractions and noises that interfere with your listening attentiveness. It may surprise you the extent to which your attention is being pulled away and splintered by distractions.

- ➤ **Next**, instead of responding immediately with your normal dominant listening style, pause a moment and make a conscious decision about what type of listening is truly appropriate and practice being flexible in the different situations you navigate.

- ➤ **Last**, be open to changing your habits and adapting your listening style and the responses you make, so they match what is happening in your present situation.

We are all very different and we naturally gravitate to different listening styles. Accountants might want to watch for the tendency to always look for the bottom line of a conversation, and lawyers might want to guard against being drawn to arguing or looking at the negative. As a business owner you may want to watch out for staying in a listening style that is too "laid back" when real problems are in need of immediate attention.

Mastering Listening Flexibility

You might be thinking now, what is my listening style, or do I even have a listening style? We all have a way of listening that becomes a comfortable habit, but we can learn to adjust and listen appropriately, if we know what listening style means. It is easy to understand, if you think of all of the different listening styles as lying on a continuum between passive and evaluative. If you imagine it laid out in this linear form, I believe you will be able to adapt and adjust your listening flexibility with more mastery.

On the passive end a person simply wants to be heard; no advice, assistance, or even sympathy need be given. The person does not need you to share an experience or say anything, all that is needed for you to do is just allow a couple of minutes for the person to be heard. On this totally passive end, it is appropriate to only offer a smile, or a nod or a slight sound.

At the evaluative end of the continuum of listening, you are expected to judge the merits of what is being said. That means making a decision about whether it is right or wrong, acceptable or unacceptable, and so forth. And after you make that decisive judgment, it is appropriate for you to follow it with substantial response and generous advice.

These examples are at the extreme ends of the listening continuum. Sometimes we do listen in these extremes; yet there is so much more, in between the passive and evaluative listening styles there is a lot of room for listening adjustment. Opportunities to listen arise every day, listen with awareness and you will know what style is needed at that moment. Practicing the following techniques will help you learn how to stretch yourself and reach for more listening flexibility.

Building Listening Flexibility

Here are five ways to improve your listening skills:

- ☞ Find a need to listen. If nothing is obvious, create a reason to listen even if you are merely giving the gift of listening.

- ☞ Always react to the ideas you hear instead of focusing superficially on the person expressing the idea.

- ☞ Concentrate on helping the other person feel like a successful communicator. You may open a path to receiving useful and enlightening information from someone you initially did not like or respect.

93

- ❧ Be open to shifting your listening style as you get a better sense of the other person's communication style, and as the message evolves during the interaction.

- ❧ Do not react to trigger words or the person's bias and attitudes. If you keep an open mind, you will recall more of the speaker's information and you will avoid the detrimental trap of overreacting.

You already adjust your listening and communication styles every day. Everyone adjusts how they speak to one another, from women and men, to children and grandparents, even employees of the same company. Throughout your life you have naturally adjusted how you listen and speak to different people. The next step is being aware of how you do it; knowing that will allow you to ease into the work of becoming a better listener.

Look around you, there are always people who want to be heard; listen to them, you may learn a lot. As you now see, the only difference in our ability to listen to each other is the motivation for true communication. If we can understand our differences, yet focus on what we have in common, we will want to communicate more powerfully and effectively.

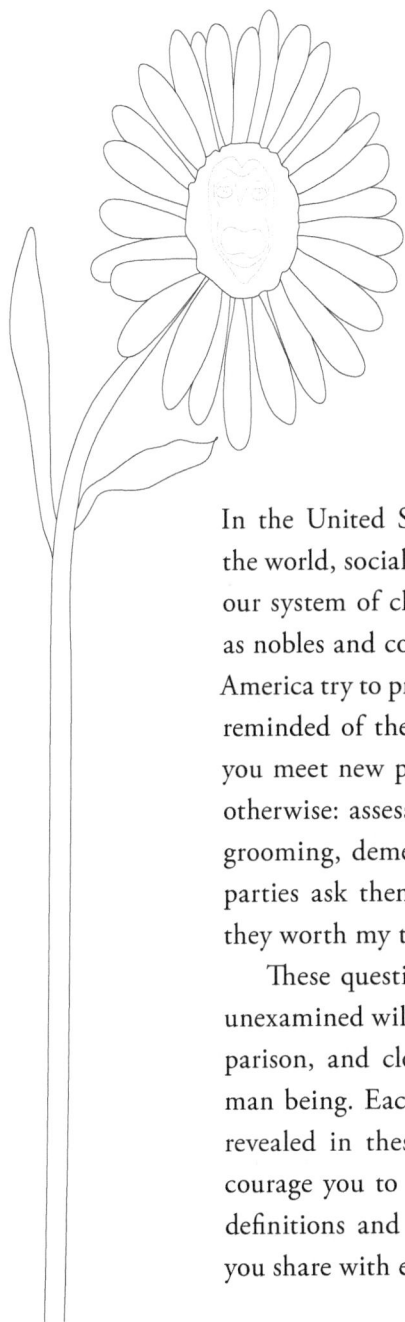

14

Class, Wealth, and All That Jazz

Navigating Socioeconomic Classes in America

In the United States as well as every other country in the world, social and economic classes divide us. Because our system of class organization is not officially defined as nobles and commoners or called a caste system, we in America try to pretend such divisions do not exist. You are reminded of the importance of this division every time you meet new people. The game begins, unconscious or otherwise: assessments are made of clothing, accessories, grooming, demeanor, and manners. And instantly both parties ask themselves, what is this person's status, are they worth my time?

These questions and answers when unconscious and unexamined will anchor you in the powerlessness of comparison, and close your mind to the value of each human being. Each person has greater depth than what is revealed in these inauthentic economic divisions. I encourage you to see beyond the limits of role and status definitions and remain open to the underlying essence you share with everyone.

Appreciating Differences in Motivation

By learning to understand the differences in role identification and motivation for each social class you will gain appreciation and realize beneficial results. I believe the capacity to comprehend the needs and appreciate the value of all groups will help you attain both your business and personal vision. I am sharing this information with you so that you can work with people from a position of empathy, even compassion. It will give you the insight to be more patient, giving, and generous, and thereby slow your own rush to judgment.

If you want to build a better business or build closer relationships with other people, understanding social differences is essential. There are distinct differences in patterns of thought and social interactions among the different economic groups. If you understand the needs and desires of all groups, you can tailor your approach to suit the innate desires of the other person. If you can understand other people and they can understand you, then there is potential for communication, and when humans connect a world of possibilities emerge. You may get what you want in business: a happy client, a successful event, or a profitable sale.

Maybe you have already identified the groups with which you plan to work, you have already positioned your company's efforts, and you are fulfilling the needs of those customers. Keep in mind, this may be too narrow, and that you are not isolated from other social groups and probably live in a community with a diverse population. Learning how to work closely with the people in these groups offers a variety of opportunities. When you consciously remove the lenses through which you view the world, your personal history, and experience, you become open to alternative views. Consciously doing this expands your creative resources and opens possibilities.

Have you noticed when your clients want to get right to the point, speak indirectly, or "chat you up" first? If you are more direct with your clients than they are with you, you could seem rude, aloof, or uncaring. You could lose them before you have barely started to develop a relationship.

Listen, be conscious, and truly tune in to the other person on all levels. When we understand the real differences between the culture and the values of our economic classes, we can move with power and ease among the social tiers and successfully fulfill our clients' desires, maneuver social events, and come closer to realizing our own dreams.

What are your customers telling you about themselves with their questions and statements? Listen carefully and you can help each person fulfill his or her desires. The following examples are from the event industry, but have you heard similar questions and statements in your line of work. "I want her to feel special." "What do other people get?" "Have you ever

96

worked with that facility?" "Can you create something new for this party?" You can learn to hear much more than just the words that are spoken.

Silent Signals and Patterns

Each economic class as well as ethnic, religious, and all other groups have silent signals, patterns, and hidden rules that help individuals live, exist, operate, or thrive in each culture. Each group has rules conveyed by a salient unspoken language that signals members of that group whether you fit in with them or do not fit in at all.

There are hidden rules about everything: food, clothing style, personal expectations, behavior, and etiquette. It is their unique combination that forms the habits and develops the signals of a group, then predictable patterns and rules evolve. Each particular group or class takes these rules for granted, and that class assumes the rules are known and followed by everyone else. Some of the problems that occur between groups arise because outsiders do not know the rules or do not realize they exist.

Normally, status within a socio-economic group is determined by a person's style. Because it is style that tells people who you are and what you think of yourself, your style is either attractive or it is not. Your style, together with your values, attitude and behavior, determines your ability to move within or between social and economic groups.

Poverty and wealth are vague measurements and exist only in relationship to each other. No amounts can be placed on them; even money is real and unreal at the same time. Status and quantities of money are fluid and can readily shift; therefore, the traits of each class may be minimized and exacerbated by a person's external support systems, such as family, friends and schools, or by internal support, intelligence, emotional stability, and spiritual stamina.

Attributes and Qualities of Socioeconomic Classes

These are very general guidelines, these are broad strokes, and they apply to economic classes irrespective of religious beliefs or racial backgrounds and ethnic history. People vary greatly and there are always many exceptions that do not fit an overarching profile, yet you will see many examples of how we accept an attribute then fallaciously claim it as who we are. The following classifications reflect roles played within group consciousness, and they do not reveal the redemptive awareness individuals are capable of achieving. Let us examine some of the adopted or inherited differences that could impact the success of your social life and business every day.

The Lower Economic Strata

Because money is lacking, people are very important to one another. This class feels a tremendous loyalty to their roots, their family, and the philosophy of their heritage. They can be very possessive of their members and there can be a tremendous defensiveness about befriending people outside their inner circle. Lacking money this group makes things happen through hard work and their relationships with each other. Moving up and out of their community would mean breaking away and abandoning their roots. This is very difficult because of their strong connections.

In poverty a person grows up learning a sense of humor is a highly valued asset, and the individual is encouraged to use his personality for entertainment. If he is highly effective at entertaining, it increases his status within the group immensely. This group is in touch with our human need for laughter, and generally all forms of entertainment are very important.

Humor is energizing. Laughter and levity are so transcendent that they elevate immune responses and endorphins, and consequently relieve stress and depression. In this group there are no social repercussions for surrendering to hilarity. A person with the ability to entertain definitely attains high status.

People living in poverty are very adept at living in the present time. Decisions are often made in the moment for the moment and are usually based on feelings of survival, relationships, and entertainment. That sentiment goes for money, too; money is to be used and spent, and if somehow a windfall occurs it is shared with others. Because they know, one day they may be in need. A typical view might be: why save? Some crisis will occur and any money saved would be used up, creating the attitude "we might as well use it now, when we need it."

Language among friends is casual and the conversation is lively. It is always participatory, exciting, and depends heavily upon gestures and other nonverbal support. Noise levels are high, and probably everyone is speaking at once. In this casual style of conversation, friends may use a vocabulary consisting of 800 words or less. As a story develops it will stop and start and jump from subject to subject before it finally gets to the point. Because there are lots of subplots and asides, the telling of the story will be quite entertaining.

To be socially included a person must be personally liked. People in this group seek acceptance through hard work and their tireless contributions to worthwhile causes. They will contribute many hours of their free time to clubs, charities, and unions doing their best to support others in their time of need.

Clothing is used as an expression of individual style and as an extension of the personality. The choices can be very interesting and unique.

Meals are social affairs and food is all about filling the belly and nourishing their loved ones. If you were a guest, your host might ask, "Did you get enough to eat?"

The Middle Class

Tools of all varieties identify the middle class, whether for the kitchen, the garage, or the business. Gadgets can proliferate. Tools enable people to produce product, and to clean and to repair equipment. If they are not available, nothing is built, repaired, or maintained. People in this group use tools and their knowledge to create a better life for themselves and for their communities. Because they take pride in making the world a better place, this group is the backbone of society; they contribute, serve, and mentor.

Things can also be very important to this class and having similar possessions with the right name brand bought at the right store helps insure the proper social fit. As a result, the personality and physical energy must be used for acquisition and maintaining stability. There is a definite keep-up-with-the-Jones race happening on many status levels of the middle class, which can add a lot of angst and economic stress. However, they are quick to open their hearts and doors to people whose lifestyles and beliefs are similar to their own.

Being safe is highly valued by the middle class, it is really the "watchword" and often the middle class citizens make their decisions by judging them against security, personal safety, and the safety of fitting into their community. Yet very often, the desire for safety leaves the middle class open to exploitation.

These attitudes create a lot of pressure to conform to common values and behavior. For that reason, rituals and rules are respected and followed, while rule breakers are marginalized. In this class it is unusual for an individual to be allowed to skip even a single bureaucratic step. Next time you are standing in line in a government office, it will be easier for you to understand the situation and what is actually happening. This will be an opportunity for you to engage your patience, listening abilities, and compassion.

People in the middle class are naturally paranoid about the norm of the status quo in which they live, because they are constantly aware of the danger of being knocked off the ladder while someone else is climbing up. Being able to climb that ladder is important because achievement and self-sufficiency are essential for inclusion.

In the middle class, people are dedicated to their work, job, or profession, and they are focused on managing their money. They are trained to project to the future and most of the time consider the future more important than the present. As a result their decisions are made against future ramifications. They understand the world from the framework that good choices made today will make a difference and can change a future for the better.

Language is used competently for negotiation. Words are chosen carefully and spoken in complete sentences; there is a lot of pride in having an excellent command of the language. In this style of using English, it is essential to get straight to the point, and be concise and clear. It is spoken not too fast or too slow; the pace will be approximately 175 words per minute, because that is the rate at which most people are the most attentive and able to comprehend your message. In keeping with the middle-class style, love and acceptance are often conditional emotions, based largely on a person's work ethic and level of achievement. Social inclusion is based to a significant degree on the quality of the individual's self-governance and his or her ability to be self-sufficient. If you want to build a successful alliance with someone in this group, you have to make that person feel secure and important. Share your ideas and plans, and some of the time let them take credit for your accomplishments; however, it is imperative to make sure they know the value of knowing you.

Clothing is often selected based on quality, label, and the extent to which it will ease acceptance into the norms of the middle class. In the same vein, quality is very important when it comes to food. There is the luxury of trying out food trends and trying new preparations. A host might ask you "Did you like it, did it taste good?"

The Wealthy Class

Wealthy people understand alliances. In the wealthy class a person uses a significant portion of his or her energy to make and maintain connections. Financial, political, and social connections are extremely valuable. Leaders in this group have mastered non-threatening techniques of persuasion and have built a constituency of people who endorse them; these attributes are the underlying support that sustains power in the wealthy class.

Legacies and pedigrees add status and although they cannot be bought, you can marry a title. Art and one-of-a-kind objects are admired and collected and often the wealthy will choose a favorite artist and be their patron as a way to promote and support the art world. Yet the wealthy conserve their money and see it as something to be protected and invested.

Language is precise and formal; words and inflection are used for networking. It is spoken at a lower register and a moderate rate of speech. Generally speaking, the higher up the chain of command in business the slower a person speaks. Because the style of communication tends to be precise, an indirect approach is the most genteel way to converse with new people in an elite class in both social and business settings. One of the most off-putting questions you can ask a sophisticated person is "what do you do?" Remember, the point is not to break the fragile bonds of new acquaintance; it is to build alliance.

Here, too, love and acceptance are conditional and closely related to social standing and connections, and there is a lot more emphasis put on social exclusion than inclusion. Tradition is more important than it would first appear because heritage and bloodlines mean more than performance. However, this group is open to newcomers who have gained high political office or new wealth through some innovation or talent. As a rule, wealthy people are generous; they are the support and backbone of non-profits everywhere.

Physical beauty, athletic prowess, and creative genius have helped actors, writers, entrepreneurs, and enterprising executives to break easily into this group. When interacting with people of wealthy means, be self-effacing, non-assuming, and do not ask direct personal questions. Above all project an aura of confidence, even if you feel you are in over your head. This is a very good time to practice your listening skills.

Clothing is seen as art; it is selected for its artistic sense and as a way to express the personality. As with other forms of art, favorite designers are patronized and their clothing is worn and valued. This same artistic style also relates to food, and how food is served and looks is very important. When you are attending a social dinner it is not so much about nutrition as it is about decorum. Wait until everyone has been served before you eat, and time yourself to finish with your host. If you were eating in a wealthy person's home you would probably not be asked whether the food was presented well, because the assumption would be that it was.

Freedom of Expression

Although it may seem odd, environments of poverty and wealth share several traits, such as a high degree of freedom of expression. I have indicated that you have to refine your behavior as you move up the social ladder, and that is mostly true, but there are significant exceptions. People will say they do not want to move up the social hierarchy because they do not want to live more constrained lives. Yes, it is necessary to hone your social skills as you move up, but nonetheless, the middle class requires the most restricting and conforming behaviors. This seems counterintuitive; however, financial independence has a way of exempting people from societal rules by which the rest of us live. A wealthy eccentric can marry eight times and so can someone on the lowest rung of society without the fear of being shunned.

Now imagine the scandal the same number of marriages would create for a person in the middle class.

Being dislodged from your station when you are at the very top or very bottom of the social strata is almost impossible. At those ends of the spectrum, there is very little movement. A sense of entitlement at the top and hopelessness at the bottom leads to freedom of expression. This is the reason that fashion trends get their start at the very top or the very bottom of the social hierarchy. Neither group depends on personal appearance for acceptance.

Introductions in Business Environments

If someone in a lower income group is introducing you, a comment will probably be made about you first. When you meet new people who are wealthy, you must have a sponsor or a person already approved by the group to make an introduction in order for you to be accepted. Yet in the middle class, to stand back and wait, and not step up and introduce yourself, is considered standoffish and even rude.

Business environments normally operate using middle-class hidden rules, signals, and values. In a business networking situation, imagine how awkward it would feel if you stood back and waited for an introduction. Have you seen that, someone waiting on the side? Do you remember how that looked and how it made you feel to watch? Also, if too many personal or intimate comments were said about you at or before a meeting it would be equally inappropriate and unacceptable. In this situation, to be successful people must know and follow the rules of middle-class negotiation and participation.

What Are You Projecting?

If you have developed an image that identifies you to a certain group, your access is limited to your peers and people in less prestigious groups. Each of us can learn to gain power and free ourselves from the restraints of our inherited culture and open many other doors for ourselves and for our businesses. Virtually no group will exclude you if you speak eloquently, dress well, and back it up with the social skills to put others at ease. What do you project now, what do you want to project, and is the natural spontaneous you shining through?

Ask yourself these important questions:

- What does my persona tell others about me?
- Am I content to be limited to this group?
- If not, what do I aspire to?

Class Mobility

There is mobility both up and down among the economic classes. Being able to move easily between groups dramatically increases your power. As a person changes income levels, new rules must be learned to operate smoothly within their new class. Generally to hasten success a person needs a spouse or mentor to model and teach them the hidden rules of the group into which they are moving.

One person can live in all three economic groups in one lifetime. Illness, death, divorce, and alcoholism can erode wealth and power. Conversely a person who has been raised in a middle-class home can be plunged into poverty after school. Then through acquiring a valuable skill or starting a successful business her income can continually increase until she moves through middle-class and into wealth. When mobility occurs, we very often retain the traits of previous classes, because they feel right to us, we are comfortable in our familiar skin. Mobility explains how traits can blur.

Broaden Your Opportunities

The case I am making is that if you wish to enter an exclusive group, you must alter your behavior to match the members of that group. It always takes a lot of self-awareness, conscious choices, and a good dose of self-discipline to reach social and professional goals. I am not advocating social climbing and I hope that is not your goal. In fact, social climbing is usually about being selfish and advancing yourself at the expense of others. You will not gain power or status by climbing over other people; it is just the opposite, this type of hostility and dishonestly weakens you and it will depress and erode your power. Also, be aware of your motives, what is your intention for entering the new group? What are you pursuing, and what is your underlying purpose for seeking admission into a targeted group of people? Always identify your motives.

Polishing your social skills and increasing your knowledge of other people will deepen your compassion and help broaden your opportunities and expand your personal power base. Even if you are happy with your current status level, the ability to be comfortable and at ease with clients and associates from several levels of society helps bring out the best in you.

Being able to successfully navigate all socio-economic groups will help you break out of your current level of success, if that is what you want. You must understand and accept the value and contributions of each social group if you are to move seamlessly among them. Denying these variations and trying to play up your own differences will only put obstacles in your way when you are trying to gain entry in new social and business environments.

There are always guards at the gate when you are trying to enter a new group. Conforming to the new group's rules is part of the passage. Give it a try; you could end up with more possibilities and freedom on the other side. Remember, you do not get the chance to show what you can do if you cannot get inside.

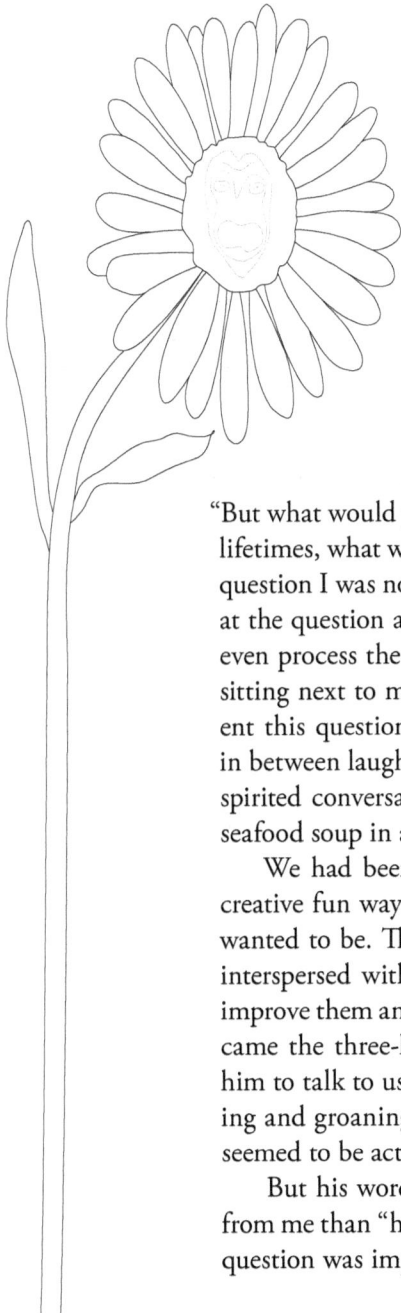

15
Meaning and Money
**Building Emotional and
Financial Resilience**

"But what would you do if you had enough money for three lifetimes, what would you do then?" When I was asked this question I was not ready to hear it. Honestly. I was stunned at the question and did not have any idea how to begin to even process the query, let alone answer it. The gentleman sitting next to me on this rainy day felt compelled to present this question to me nonetheless. His question drifted in between laughter and Animal Planet and a light-hearted spirited conversation my husband and I were having over seafood soup in a Costa Rican hotel bar.

We had been talking about business and money and creative fun ways to make more of it in places we actually wanted to be. These dreams we were speaking about were interspersed with talk of our own businesses and how to improve them and change them to make more money. Then came the three-lifetimes question. It was not unusual for him to talk to us; people were joining in, we were all laughing and groaning at Animal Planet. The place was alive, it seemed to be actually jumping.

But his words could not elicit any more of a response from me than "huhh." I was not ready to hear them, but the question was implanted in my mind, and his words lurked in the recesses of my memory for a very long time. That evening I was polite, conversational, and at the same time completely dumbstruck. At home, it was months before I thought of him again, and even longer before I understood how profound his question had been. Yet even the first time I heard myself say "Oh that's what that guy was talking about," I still did not get it. But I was beginning to understand the importance of the question, and now I have come to think of this gentleman as the equivalent of a messenger angel.

Money and Enlightenment

Does it take money to become enlightened? Exploring the answer to this question is essential to understanding our relationship with money and how money relates to adding meaning to our lives. After the basic needs of food and shelter are met, our search for meaning begins. We use money to enjoy simple human pleasures and participate in activities that utilize our creativity. Both of these ways of using money can nourish us and help us to feel our lives are well lived. And yes, money helps.

For the most part, at least a modicum of money allows you the time, space, and freedom to participate in activities that speak to you and engage you completely. When you are fully engaged, you are enmeshed in the present of what you are doing; you lose the perspective of time and space. Losing a sense of time and space creates a state called flow, a momentary experience of eternity. Do you remember saying "I was in the flow," when everything was going your way? Flow creates a timelessness, a sense of being present that is very close to enlightenment. In fact, in some forms it mimics the transcendent states of enlightenment described by mystics of all religious faiths.

You need money for everything. Even if you go on retreat you generally need money to get there, unless you are relying on the kindness of strangers and their money. You will need money for shelter, food, and spiritual offerings. Even if you sleep outside, you will need a blanket or a sleeping bag, maybe a tent and ground cover. Everything requires money.

Now the obvious question might be: is money essential to find spiritual awakening, do you need money to be enlightened? The question is rhetorical, yet you also know that money permeates nearly every aspect of your life.

Happiness and Money

Money and living well are forever entwined. Yet having money will not ensure your life is well lived. It does not just automatically happen that you live your life well and wisely if you have money. You have to draft your life by the way you focus your intentions and plan your activities, so that you live your life by design not default. Ask yourself "am I living the life I want to live, do I get up in the morning with zest, excited about a new day? Would I be doing the job I'm doing, if it weren't for the money?"

Since childhood we have heard the saying "money doesn't buy happiness." We tend to think it does, however, and we put the two words together a lot. When we see others who have more than us, one might suspect they are happier and that a little more money will make us a little happier too, and a lot more money will make us a lot happier. We even look to money to solve problems money cannot solve.

The reality is that unless you are buying yourself out of a cardboard box and into an apartment, with more money you are not likely to be any happier. Normally your debt ratio will merely increase proportionate to your income, maybe your debt will even surpass your income. Having greater amounts of money only buys different types of problems. Sai Baba noticed this, he said, "When you pile up riches, fear and anxiety are also piling up in proportion."

I believe it is our birthright to live happy, prosperous lives, and I believe this can involve a lot more money coming into our lives. Accomplishing this means understanding our relationship with money as a sacred energy and becoming aware of what money can and cannot give us. It is easy to waste money, we have all done it, but when we do, it is like squandering our vitality. Our ability to use our money wisely depends heavily on our ability to actively do the following:

- Release grudges.
- Engage forgiveness.
- Focus on finding what is meaningful.
- Appreciate the bounty of small pleasures.
- Understand our talents and expand them.

Letting go of grudges, being forgiving, and grateful are not normal money topics because they have nothing to do with consuming products. Consuming is what we normally think of when we think of money. Yet we can also use our money to develop our strengths and to participate in the activities we love with people we care about. To do this it takes a change in perspective from our contemporary consumptive view of money and spending, to seeing money as a resource and using it sensibly and with awareness. Can money buy happiness? It buys happiness when it wisely serves your practical and spiritual needs, plus the needs of others. Use your money with discernment and you will employ its power to design your life.

Right Livelihood

What if you do not have enough money for three lifetimes? What if you have bills to pay, and food to buy, how do you live a meaningful life then? Most of us cannot just drop everything to find ourselves and take off on a trip around the world, go to the desert, or live in a monastery. We need to integrate a life of meaning while we take care of the responsibilities and basic realities of our lives, and this means making money. It is not an impossible task to put meaning and money together; however to do so, it takes focusing your energy and participating fully in your human experience.

When you are working in a job you love and you are making money, you are in Right Livelihood. If the love is missing or the money is missing, then what you are doing is not right for you. If you know your work is wrong for you, staying there three or five more years will not make it right.

The love of your work and the income that sustains you entwine to build a great life. Even a job you love has really icky moments, but do they overwhelm the good of it? Only you can answer. It is possible to engage the powerful energy that surrounds money and use it to assist you, support you, and work for you while doing a job you love.

This happens naturally when you engage the power of your intelligence and time, and then take control of your thinking and actions. I am not suggesting you can simply affirm your way to wealth. I am saying your thoughts and actions need to be pursuant to what you want to manifest. Normally you are not going to do that from the isolation of your living room; you need to get out and interact with people in your community and beyond. Get up, go out, face your fear of the murky waters, and make it happen; be yourself and use this practical information to maneuver in what is often an unenlightened world.

Put in the effort to find work you love, or find a way to honestly love your work; this action will help you to build personal wealth without angst and worry, and gain respect for the energy money holds. One of the keys to financial stability is understanding that financial resilience is always intertwined with emotional resilience. These are the two underpinnings essential to moving smoothly through life. Being grounded and at home with yourself is crucial to knowing you are capable of taking care of yourself and surviving in the world.

Money and Fear

Are you afraid of being alone and poor? If so take heart, you are not alone. This is one of the common fears that binds humanity together. There is a lot of angst and concealment around money, and because of these dark emotions, we do not really want to look at the power money holds over us.

Because of the innate nature of secrecy and anxiety, we do things for money that we would never dream of doing otherwise. We stay in jobs we hate for the sake of financial security, when every fiber of our being is screaming, run. We spend money on things we cannot afford so it will appear we have more money than we do. We even make investments we know are too "good to be true."

It is natural to feel anxiety around money because money, by definition, is finite. Money is not alone in this attribute, it shares this characteristic with all our other assets; they are limited too. We only have so much time and energy, and there is always a limit to our personal effectiveness. Not one thing in our physical world is limitless, and whether we realize it or not our subconscious is aware of it all the time, keeping track, counting, and watching. The awareness of forests being cut, wells running dry, and lives being cut short are embedded in our collective memory as the condition of scarcity. We have seen money run out, we have seen love run out, and we know time is running out. This knowledge of scarcity and the fear that accompanies it is one of the conditions that is shared by all of humanity.

But, interestingly, amassing more money will not get to the basic root of this innate human fear. If you only measure your success by how much money you have, you will always feel deprived, because as you amass more, you shift your focus onto what you do not have, and what you do not have is empty like a big growing black hole. A study focusing on wealthy people in Australia states that only about 5% of those well-to-do households view themselves as prosperous. Half said their financial situations were reasonably comfortable, and a significant portion viewed themselves as just getting by.

Never Enough

If you define your success on how much money you are piling up, you become more focused on how finite your pile is. Normally, when you make more, you spend more, and your debt load expands proportionately. Then, the part of you who understands scarcity grows larger too. This happens because you compare yourself to a greater and greater extent with other people who have more money, and it is a fact of life that there will always be other people with more money, a bigger house, and more toys than you.

Consequently, the more your attachment to money grows, the more your fear of scarcity becomes apparent. This is not just true of wealthy people; when people who earned considerably less money were studied, it was found they too have the same relationship of attachment and fear. We cannot escape this, because the very nature of our human experience is one of limitation. But our awareness of this snare will weaken its influence and lessen the grip it has on our reactions.

When you only focus on making more money, more money will never be reached, because "more money" is a fantasy. You can continue to grasp for it, but you can never reach enough of it. If you set your vision to make more money, and your only goal is the money, your life becomes a hollow and empty experience, because enough money is never attained.

As you put your financial picture together, keep in mind, it is always the emotion behind the money and the comfort money buys that makes money worth having. If you keep your eye on the emotion around money, you will access the power money holds. If you forget this and reach for the money itself, the search physically depletes you, your personal power continually drains, and over time your energy completely scatters. Paradoxically, each of us intuitively knows that continually pushing for more is inherently frustrating, but when it comes to money, we forget what we know.

Given that we know our life is limited, and the scarcity of all our other resources is a fact also, it is evident that fear is an inherent part of who we are and our behavior. Therefore, I am suggesting that we need to embrace this and accept it. Because the more we try to deny it and push it back and cover it up, the more scarcity, limitation, and restriction shows up in our lives.

Limitations are part of what makes us human. Of course we are imperfect, yet we are perfect in all our imperfection; our shortcomings are guides on the human journey. Totally accepting your faults and limitations like they are comfortable old friends coming to visit you, puts you at ease with yourself. When you are self-assured and at ease, other people can sense it and they are drawn to you, want to be with you, and mirror you. Being at ease has the capacity to increase your consciousness and vitality and it is a very attractive quality. When you are at ease, you help others relax and put them at ease also.

Total Acceptance

It is possible to accept your fear of things running out without the fear paralyzing you and holding you in place. Because you know that your life is limited, it makes it all that much more precious and beautiful. The same is true of money: because you know it is limited, the wise use of this cherished resource can bring you even greater joy and fulfillment.

Being able to accept emotions as they enter and pass through your being gives you the resilience to handle all of them without getting tangled up and caught in them. In your life you will experience grief and joy, anxiety and beauty—everything you need to practice acceptance, the good along with the bad. There is a lot of power in actively accepting everything that comes your way. If you resist anything in your life, you are resisting the natural energy flow of your life. This includes the flow of love and money. When you emotionally close up and shut down, love also closes up and shuts down. Your energy gets bound up, your strength and vitality get bound up and just like everything else, your money also gets bound up.

Yet, paradoxically, the moment you accept everything your human experience has to offer, you are immediately able to accept more. This means examining and surrendering to all of it, including the fear and the despair, along with the hope and the levity. The very moment you clear your heart by accepting who you are, is the minute you are saying yes to life. When you do this, you are saying yes to abundance, and once you say yes to abundance, you are able to attain prosperity.

Accepting prosperity into your life means totally accepting your accomplishments as well as your failures. Sometimes it is easier to admit your shortcomings than claim your achievements. Practice accepting and congratulating yourself just like a good friend would recognize you. Your acceptance integrated with what you truly want will magnetically propel you to the right job and attract prosperity. Remember, when you are going against the flow of life, you can put in a lot of hours, work really hard, and get nowhere.

Just like all resources, money's natural state is ebb and flow. If you have been experiencing the flowing out perspective rather than the flowing in side of money, take a good look at yourself. What are you missing? What are you resisting? Are you doing the right work for you? Open up, wake up and see what it might be.

Unfinished Money Business

Each one of us has unfinished money business; however, some of us have let this work grow into a large mountain that seems out of control. Incomplete tasks around money always begin to permeate the rest of your life. This incomplete money business affects how your office looks, how your house looks, and how you feel about yourself.

Even though you may have let this work pile up, the good news is you can begin immediately to get control of it. Observe where you have been lax with money and let your good intentions slip into consciousness and let your awareness dissolve your bad habits. Once you start to work on your relationship with money, you will see improvement quickly.

When you looked at this list did you feel any tightness in your body because you see yourself in these questions? Have you thought about your conscientiousness and how it affects your prosperity? Returning things you have borrowed and paying your debts is basically the same thing, and there

---

Weighted questions

All the questions below hold significance and are weighted financial questions. That is, each one has the power to bind you in place, as if you were chained by a heavy lead weight.

- ❧ Do you owe money to family members or friends?
- ❧ Do you have high balances on your credit cards?
- ❧ Do you lose receipts or do not keep track of your expenses?
- ❧ Do you have overdue books or movie rentals?
- ❧ Does your business have enough liability insurance?
- ❧ Are your financial records in order and in places you can find them?
- ❧ What service people do you owe?
- ❧ Where do you stand in your preparations for retirement?
- ❧ What person or people do you blame for your money problems?

---

is a direct correlation between paying your debts and whether or not you collect the money people owe you.

Take a piece of paper. List the areas where you have created a financial mess. Start with the easiest thing on the list and begin to work on it immediately, then put a time and date on each of the other items that you intend to complete.

As you begin to return things you have borrowed and to pay the people you owe, you will gain more energy in your life. You will also find it easier to stop unconscious spending. When you clean up your unfinished money business, you will find you are not as worried about your past or your future, because you have eliminated a nagging worry and patched an energy drain that is constantly leaking from you, stealing your vitality. You will be freer to direct your power and energy to areas where you want to use it.

Being responsible with money also means keeping track of where you spend money. You may decide you are going to keep track of everything over $1 if you have a lot of debt, or $5 or $10 if you do not. Whichever you choose, make it a habit to track how you use your currency, and truly understand your relationship to money.

If you are not responsible with money, you know it and your subconscious knows it too. When you spend money on things that bring you joy and meaning it is very rewarding. Think of a time when you spent "good money" on a meal in a restaurant where the food was delicious, but the company miserable. How did you feel then? Everything needs to be in place to feel your money is well spent. When you feel wasteful, it is difficult for you to attract more money. You intuitively know this about the power and energy that surrounds money. Put what you already know to work.

One More Comment on Forgiveness

Who do you still need to forgive? Are you willing to consider that your attachment to past pain and grievance is holding you back? Keeping you from getting what you want? Even if you are not quite willing to forgive yet, just considering that it is possible to forgive will put a gap between you and the grudge. Holding a grudge does just that, it puts you into a holding pattern. Is that what you want? Listen carefully to what author Ron Smothermon said, "Forgiving someone is solid proof of your intent to live your life now, while you still have it." Ponder what these words mean to you.

You may have been lied to or lied about. You may have had your money stolen, and even your hope stolen, for a time. But do you want to be energetically tied to the person who inflicted the suffering? Forgiveness is an act of will and a journey into courage. Holding a grudge takes focus and effort and steals your energy and vitality. When you forgive you are being compassionate and generous to yourself. It releases you to use your bound-up energy for prosperity.

Curing Hiccups?

When I was a child my Uncle Ralph taught my Cousin Diane and I how to initiate the hiccups. We followed his instructions, carefully going through all the steps he laid out for us. Sure enough we gave ourselves a case of the hiccups. Now the problem was, once we had the hiccups, we wanted to get rid of them. However, all of the solutions were coming up short, and the hiccups seemed to go on and on. We drank water, held our breath, and tried standing on our heads. One thing we did not try was money.

One day when my friend Rita was visiting from Maine, I watched her pull a $10 bill out of her purse and offer it to my son, who had a case of the hiccups. All Simon had to do was give her one more hiccup and he could have the money. It seemed like an easy thing to do, but with the $10 bill in front of him he could not produce another hiccup, and Simon did not get the money. Rita told me that she has never bought one hiccup.

Since then I have made it a personal mission to try to buy a hiccup. I have waved a $20 dollar bill and I have offered as little as a single $1 dollar bill, but I always keep my money. Is it possible that money is so powerful it can cure the hiccups? What else could money do for you, if you would just let it into your life?

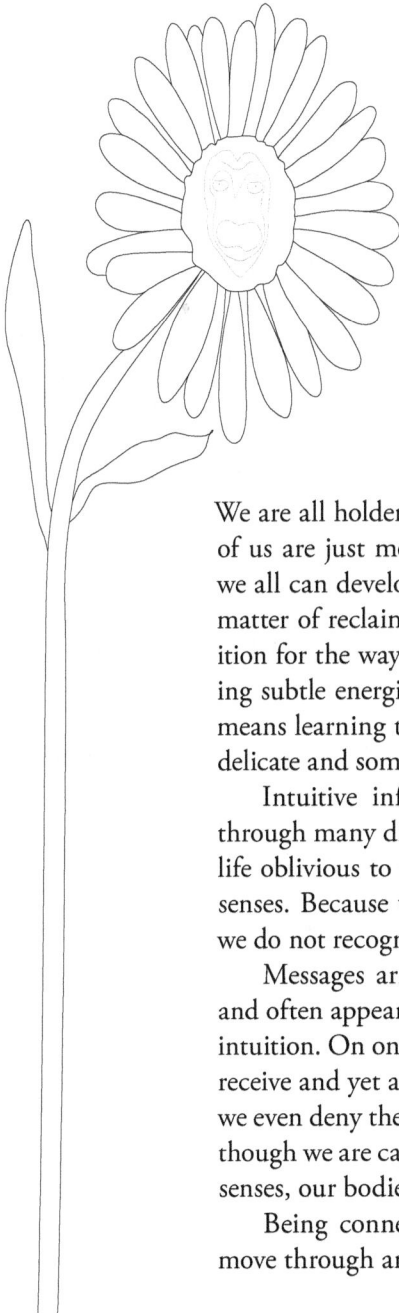

16
Connecting With Intuition
How to Revive This Natural Source of Power in You

We are all holders of an innate intuitive intelligence. Some of us are just more aware of it; we are born intuitive and we all can develop it throughout our entire lifetime. It is a matter of reclaiming our natural history and refining intuition for the way we live now. We are constantly experiencing subtle energies. Developing our intuitive selves merely means learning to read and interpret the language of these delicate and sometimes elusive subtle energies.

Intuitive information is coming to us all the time, through many different avenues, yet most of us go through life oblivious to the messages knocking at the door of our senses. Because we have ignored the messages for so long, we do not recognize intuition when we are receiving it.

Messages arrive suddenly, sometimes out of nowhere, and often appear to be illogical. This can be the paradox of intuition. On one level we believe the ideas and inklings we receive and yet at the same time doubt them; paradoxically we even deny their very existence. We cannot stop intuition, though we are capable of ignoring it as it comes through our senses, our bodies, and our thoughts, at least for a time.

Being connected to your intuition requires that you move through and beyond acceptance of your life and into compassion. A working street definition of compassion is this: being able to hold different beliefs in your mind at once and know it. If you are open to these perceptions, it will expand your idea of what it means to be alive and to live the human experience.

Always have compassion for your efforts and mistakes, your shortcomings and challenges, and have compassion for the enormous amount of energy you expend at living, learning, and doing the things you do every day. You even need compassion for the effort and intention it takes to let go of entrapments, and settle into the simplicity it requires to connect with the feelings in your body that speak to you as your intuition.

The Language of Intuition

Intuition is a language that connects the body and the mind. Being able to tap into the power of intuition helps us to live better and happier lives today, understand our past, and be more successful in the future. The language of intuition can be seen as a dialog between the mind and the body. Some see intuition as a dialog between divine consciousness and the human soul. You will recognize intuition through insights and subtle suggestions that will come to you in seemingly illogical ways. Yet each perspicacity can have marked accuracy.

In order to connect with this power and focus on the energy of intuition, you need to realize that intuition comes to you in the form of physical sensations involving emotions. As an example, imagine this situation: you are at home and you are getting ready to leave. All at once you feel a tightness in your stomach, and something is telling you not to leave yet. So you think, "I shouldn't leave without getting more of my chores done." You begin to do them, but then 10 minutes later the phone rings, and the caller gives you vital information that will insure the success of a project you are working on.

Is this just a coincidence? Maybe, but you have had similar experiences. You recognize the example because you can relate to the response. You have had the experience of receiving information at the precise moment you needed it, and precisely when you could act on it. At other times you may have had sensations in your body and felt an inkling to act, and you did not respond. What did you miss then? You will never know.

Coming to Your Senses

Intuition is an internal way of knowing about the world. It is a way of perceiving the world using a combination of your senses with greater awareness. When you use your intuition, you integrate all the senses; it is only the pattern of integration that is unique to each person. Intuition is an asset common to everyone; it is only how each person receives and uses the information that differs.

You may be asking yourself, "Me, am I intuitive?" The answer is yes. You receive messages in your body through smell, sight, sound, and sensations; there are many ways to perceive. Intuition may come to you merely as a nagging no, do not buy this item, do not hire this person. Conversely, notice when you feel positive about something throughout your body.

Although the pragmatic world may renounce the resource of intuition on one level, on another level, hunches have always been a part of business environments. Business innovation would never happen if an idea did not first start as a hunch. The hunch becomes an evolving idea integrated with thought processes; it is investigated, pursued and developed as a plan. But, it still started as intuition disguised as a hunch.

Obviously there is a lot of personal power in connecting with intuition. If we can gain so much by using this energy, why is it that so few of us are developing and cultivating our intuitive intelligence?

Of course the answer is, we do not really think we are intuitive. We think intuition is for other people. Many times intuition is confused with clairvoyance and mysticism. It appears to us that if we do not have this type of intuition, then we must not have any intuition at all. However, if we judge ourselves against this extreme version of knowing about the world, then we cannot recognize our own language of intuition because we are not open to observing it.

Also we think that every time we have acted on a hunch, and it worked out for us, we were merely lucky. We suppress our intuitive nature, because, if we did believe in intuition, we would be giving in to the deeply seated, insidious notion that we would have to be out of our minds.

Eliminating "Dis-Ease"

Even though each one of us believes in a lot of things we cannot see, it is difficult to believe intuition is something that can be cultivated. Yet it can be, because it rests in our bodies, and is carried by our senses. It flows naturally over the bridge between mind and body when we are open to all of our emotions, each one that passes through us. This dialog then guides us to make wise and productive decisions for our lives.

But what happens when you do not face your emotions? Is it merely that you do not become intuitive? The consequence is that unacknowledged and buried emotions become embedded in the body. Your unobserved and undefined emotions, and the emotions you have pushed back and have not dealt with, cross the bridge from your mind to your body and are stored in your organs, where they rest, waiting for a possible chemical or biological assault.

Western medicine acknowledges the mind-body connection, and its presence is receiving more attention. But our discussion and work with intuition and power is not one of disease, it is of dis-ease. It is about how ignoring, or handling your emotions poorly, and not developing your self-knowledge and awareness can stop you from getting what you want, finding love, connecting with money, connecting with intuition, and making the most of your life.

Why wait for illness or disappointment to tell you that you are stuck and not pursuing the life of your dreams? If you can be open to change and the subtle messages you are receiving, you could be open to a whole lot more in your life. You might even be able to implement subtle adjustments early, and avoid having to endure a lot of trauma and disappointment in your life.

The Flow of Intuition

Although it is hard to accept the more negative emotions, allowing yourself to do so gives you the opportunity to see there is always another side to every emotion. For instance, anger is a very important emotion; it warns us of danger and it can be vital in protecting us. It is how we act on the anger that is crucial. Does the action you take when you are angry open up a broader world to you, does it bring you closer to people, solve problems, and get you what you want? Or does it undermine your happiness, knock you off the path to success, and weaken your personal power?

On the other hand, kindness can be a trap, too. When you put your efforts into trying to be kind and spiritual, you can get trapped in the trying and the effort. You are a whole person and being kind and spiritual is part of it, not the whole of it. Do not repress any part of yourself, or reject what you see as unflattering. If you deny even a small piece of you, you will deny the intrinsic human experience and you will delay learning the intuitive process.

Each of us knows what it feels like to be picky, derisive, fed-up, unmerciful, and exceedingly impatient. Of course, none of us want to think of ourselves as being like that; still, I am suggesting that you let these feelings flow through you. When you feel them well up, be simply aware, let them pass by without getting stuck in your body or latching onto your mind.

Compassion and Connection

When you have compassion for yourself, your fears, your faults, and for everything that it means to live the human experience, you can shift your perspective and become more relaxed in life, then the process of connecting with your natural intuition begins. Having compassion for yourself gives you a model, a success pattern for having compassion for other people. When awareness is applied, this is a cycle that can continue to repeat itself and compassion can become a habit.

But the truth is, even if you are still engaged in thoughts or acts of revenge and treachery or feel locked in some such cycle, if you choose to be self-aware and pause long enough, you will receive intuitive hits about the deleterious effects of your actions. This occurs since it is your nature to be perceptive and seek wholeness. I can also assure you, revenge and other negative impulses are based in fear, and fear and negativity will block the growth of your intuition.

Fear comes to us directly from our ancestors; we are their descendants because they reacted to fear appropriately, which enabled them to save their lives. Yet fear is a state of mind that easily becomes a habit that does not serve you. If you have become habituated to fear and any of the negative emotions it breeds, you need not remain that way. This is another opportunity for using the art of substitution, replacing the positive for the negative. Releasing fear is not easy; however, neither is living a fearful life.

The Road to Intuition

Believing in yourself and your ability to cultivate intuition starts the process. Your belief actually separates you from your fear and negativity and it creates a space for intuition to grow. Thoughtfully envisioning yourself as an intuitive, compassionate person sets you up to be successful at interpreting your own intuitive language.

I am suggesting that you decide to see yourself as courageous, loving, and wise from the very beginning of this journey. Also, see yourself as growing into an easy power that is based within you, and know this is an energy influenced by you. With practice, you will become a better observer of your emotions. If you can become the observer, rather than the reactor, analyzer, and judger of your experience, you will be a better participant in your life.

Three assets to develop are desire, belief, and willingness:

    ℞ **Desire**: Consider the many advantages of being intuitive. Imagine how it can support you in your decision-making, giving you valuable insights and supporting your intelligence and your acquired knowledge, to help you make better choices.

 ↪ **Belief**: Recognize the ways your intuitive nature has helped you in the past. Then believe in your ability to continue to develop a better understanding of your power and energy.

 ↪ **Willingness**: Be willing to try the exercises. They can heighten your awareness of subtle energies that surround you. Also be willing to incorporate the practice of being aware of these energies as you go about your everyday life.

Integrating Your Personal Enduring Traits

For you to become aware of how intuition can be integrated into your life, you can begin by looking at what you have already discovered about yourself. I would like for you to go back to Chapter 2 and look at the responses you developed there. When you look at your answers from your present perspective, is it easier to understand the reasoning behind your attraction to the attributes of certain people?

Begin looking at the traits and qualities of the people you now admire. Their surface traits are most obvious, and they are still important, but if you look behind the surface traits, you will see the enduring traits. They are really the true qualities that subtly attracted you to the person. Enduring traits are the attributes and energies that tell you from the "heart of your being" who you truly are. They tell you that you want to be a good parent, a supportive sister, a steadfast friend, and so forth. They tell you that you want to be brave, adventurous, optimistic, insightful, or successful.

There are many enduring traits and you already possess several. Enduring traits lie beneath and show themselves through your interactions with others and in how you live your life. They are visible in your desires and longings. One of the reasons we as a species can have so much sadness in our lives is because we are not in touch with our own enduring traits. Had you been interested in why you were drawn to the people you chose?

How did you say you wanted to use your time? How closely do your seven favorite things match your enduring traits? You will first notice the things that delight you, bring you joy, and light a spark in you. Also notice what makes you angry and what you want to dismiss; these may also be qualities intrinsic to your soul.

Examine yourself carefully; look for your deeper truth, the truth that lies beneath the surface.

It is obvious that one of the reasons you even noticed the people you chose is because you identified with them. Even though you may think you do not possess those qualities and intentions, you do, or you have the potential to possess them. Let your new awareness open a bigger space in you for those attributes to grow. They will take root, and they will grow strongly.

Living Up to Your Potential

When you identify the intention behind the desire for what you want, you identify what is really driving you. It is then that you can bring forth the traits you already have. This is part of what it means to live up to your human potential. Do you remember your parents and teachers telling you that you were not living up to your potential? As a child I always wondered what my potential was, but the concept of potential and purpose was never explained to me, at least not in a way I understood. My parents were busy taking really good care of me, but the topic of how to use intuition to search for the meaning of my life did not come up. That sort of thing was never discussed.

What stops you from getting in touch with your potential and your life's purpose? Do you think it is silly, simplistic, or stupid to look at how intuition has helped you? Has your mind played around with such thoughts? Your intellect will only take you so far and your mind playing around with low-energy negative ideas or cynical thoughts can stop you from pursing a truly meaningful, successful, and happy life.

Actually the true cost of not being purposeful, not living congruently, and not going after what you want is living a life that leads to anxiety and frustration. This is way too high of a price to pay. Become aware of your possibilities and act when necessary, because what merely rests within your potential, will give you nothing.

Exercises for Awakening Intuition

As you start the exercises, it will be helpful to have an idea of where your comfort zone lies along the continuum of ambiguity. Are you comfortable with uncertainty, or are you more at ease when you know precisely how an event will unfold? How do you feel when you do not understand the meaning and content of what is happening? Are you able to let the context of the event paint a more complete picture later? Take a look at your thoughts and emotions concerning uncertainty, where do you naturally lie on the ambiguity continuum?

A person can welcome ambiguity in some areas and not in others, For example, there is no room for ambiguity in the work of air traffic controllers, yet in their private lives they may be comfortable with quite a bit of vagueness and uncertainty. Also, it is advantageous for an Internist to be knowledgeable, flexible, and comfortable when treating people since human beings can react to medicines, bee stings, or trauma in a wide variety of ways. There is no one right place to be, comfort with ambiguity will adjust over a day and over a lifetime. The idea is to know where you are at any given moment.

Start by examining where you naturally lie along that continuum, then go for some more flexibility. Examine concepts you now see as fixed. What does it mean to you to be a wife, a brother, to be safe, to be civil, to be happy, or be beautiful? Have you decided for yourself? Normally, all of these concepts are mental constructs developed within community, and they are ambiguous and change over time. The following exercises are important because they help you get in touch with your intuition through your own nature and your own body and soul, not through other people.

Exercise #1: Belly Laughter

Laughter can be like sorbet, cleansing your palette between the courses of life. It can be a stopgap in the midst of sorrow. Just the action of laughter alters your body. You do not even have to be happy to get the benefits of laughter. Of course happiness and laughter can go together, but they do not have to. Laughter immerses the systems of your body in positive vibrations, especially when you let your whole body shake.

When you allow yourself the healthy relief of laughter during the troubles that come to you just because you are human, in that moment you can allow intuition to enter. If you let your guard down as you crack up in laughter, intuition seeps in through the breaks in your anxiety, giving you creative hits on how to proceed.

You have probably read articles and literature about how laughter relieves stress, anxiety, and heals the body by elevating the normal response of the human immune system. Undoubtedly, you have had the experience of feeling better after laughing. Go deeper, remember, many times during or immediately following laughter you have also received creative ideas, which you then implemented in your life. At this moment can you remember some of them? It happens so naturally that you will often overlook these intuitive hits and the benefits you gain. Be conscious because these creative moments are yours to expand and explore.

Look for ways to laugh and look for things to laugh about; humor is all around you. Go to a comedy club, watch the comedy channel, or rent a funny movie. If you are not sure which movie is funny, ask a friend who laughs. In fact, make it a point to spend your time with people who laugh. You will learn to laugh more too, and you will also create that necessary break in routine thought that is needed to make space in your life for intuition to enter.

Laughter will make you more creative and intuitive, and you will benefit by feeling much better too. Children know this instinctively; they do and say silly things just to laugh. I know a child who walks up to me and says, "Let's laugh." And we laugh. She is in touch with how laughter makes her feel. A five-year-old laughs 250 times a day – that is our lifetime peak, from there our daily laughter continues to fall. You can re-create child-like laughter in your life. Look for humor, say silly things, and let the ideas flow. What did you love as a child? Maybe you can laugh at those memories right now. I particularly appreciate Shirley MacLaine's comment, "The person who knows how to laugh at himself will never cease to be amused."

Exercise #2: Engage Relaxation

As a community we have fallen into the routine of filling up every moment of each day. It has become a badge of honor to be incredibly busy. We even spend our down time in frenetic activity, with a cell phone to our ears, or device in our hands, often we have no idea who we are walking by. Personally, I know this is a very difficult habit to break, because over-scheduling is a problem for me, too.

It is also possible to be present when you are working, in fact your presence acts as conduit for productivity and intuitive insight. Yet it is in the moments when we are quiet and truly present—when we relax, meditate, pray, or pay attention to our breath—that we can synthesize everything we are receiving and contemplate its meaning. You may be wondering if you have enough time to do this. But even as that thought passes through your mind, you already know you have to make the time for stillness.

By taking very good care of yourself and purposefully scheduling relaxation, you will give intuition a chance to seep through in the moments of quiet. It does not take long—10 seconds or 1 minute of quiet and stillness will give you the opportunity to experience transcendence. These moments of quiet and relaxation are when your connection with intuition is initiated and your creativity is expanded.

Moments of transcendence can also be found while actively listening to music, getting a massage, or indulging in self-care. Taking the time for a luxurious bath takes you out of rushing and places you into the serene space of personal time. Your life is a precious gift that lasts only a short time, take the time to enjoy it and care for yourself. Connecting with the joy of taking very good care of yourself empowers you; it lifts your self-esteem, and high self-esteem gives you the confidence to listen to your intuition.

Be prepared, take note, because it always happens that when you begin to simplify your life and relax more, your resolve will be challenged. Your commitment to resting and developing your intuition will be tested, you will be asked to do more, to add more stuff into your life. Without a doubt, someone always appears with a very attractive request. How will you respond when you are tempted?

Exercise #3: Practice Empathy

Being able to put yourself in another person's shoes, to "walk a mile in them" as the saying goes, opens you to their experience. The ability to see the world from another's perspective opens your mind and heart to receiving an incredible amount of information.

Have you had the experience of just not wanting to see the other person's side of things? Remember how closed off you felt? Have you made being closed off a pattern of behavior? You can change that. When you imagine yourself in another's experience, you will receive an impression or get a glimpse of it. The more you practice empathy, the greater will be your understanding of your personal intuitive language. Put yourself in another person's place, imagine what he or she is feeling, and notice how you perceive. Are you seeing it, are you hearing it, how are you sensing the messages you are receiving?

If you become very good at intuitive empathy, be careful not to take on the negative burdens of other people into your own body. Being able to suffer with another person for the moment is a gift to both you and them. However, let it be for just the moment, because it is possible to become terribly weighted down by another's experience, if you take empathy to the extreme. You can learn a lot from empathy when your heart is open to it; use it wisely.

Exercise #4: Go to the Grocery Store

Intuition is for everyday life. Therefore, practice it in your everyday activities as you go to work and do your errands. You will become enlightened in the experience and you will learn how much intuition enhances your abilities.

When you are in the grocery store it is easy to stand close to people without being too intrusive. You can comfortably stand next to people at the deli counter, the bakery section, and the checkout line. Try to pick up a general impression and to sense the energy of the people near you. Try to let the feelings flow through you, do not be judgmental or jump too quickly to fixed conclusions. Relax, be perceptive, and above all do not try too hard. You are practicing and being available for insight, impressions, and intuition.

Push your cart throughout the entire produce section. To which fruit and vegetables are you attracted? Some food will attract you and draw you closer. Place your hand about 2" over the top of each food item. What vibrations do you feel? Do you feel any? Proceed on to the meat counter and again, hold your hand over the top of the different meats, you will still get some sensations through the plastic. Which variety or cuts attract you? Then intuitively choose the foods you feel will nourish your own body the best.

Next, take your food home and prepare it. After you have eaten the food you have chosen, do you feel energized or depleted? Do you feel the food was alive or dead? Think about and meditate on the choices you made at the grocery store. Do you feel your choices were correct and your intuition helped you?

Exercise #5: Try Being in a Big Crowd

Groups of people who gather together emanate a mood also. One music festival may lift you out of your normal state of being and transcend you to an altered state of consciousness where you lose track of time and space. Another may ground you in an earthy reality. Notice that it is never just the music, it is the people and the event too. Everything radiates a vibration.

Check out what it feels like to be in crowds at shopping malls, art fairs, and sporting events; each will have its own mood. Do you find them sedate, dull, lively, or scary? What sensations are you noticing in your body at the different events? Are you energized? Are you depleted? This is part of your work in understanding your own language of intuition. Again, always protect yourself, even if you are energized at an event, it is not unusual to need some alone time after engaging with a large group of people.

Put Intuition to Work in Your Life

Loosening your body with laughter, relaxing instead of rushing, and opening yourself to feeling what you feel without judgment opens you to intuition. Does this sound too simplistic to you? Intuition is common sense in a simple and spontaneous form; this is why our natural instinctive way of knowing can easily be disregarded.

My brother Bob is an archeologist. During his first job, with only an undergraduate degree, he found many remarkable sites. When I asked him how he was able to do this, he replied, "Pam, a good place, is a good place, is a good place. If you recognize it, then somebody who lived long before you recognized it too." At that time, even though we did not talk about it, it appears my brother was connected to his intuition and used it effectively in his job. However as he become more educated and earned his Masters Degree and then his PhD, for a time he devalued his own intuitive nature. Like many other experts he became attached to his scientific training, and only believed in what could be concretely proved. But the fundamental sense of intuition always seeps back in as you become confidant. My brother is no exception, when I asked him about his use of intuition, he admitted it was alive and assimilated into his work. We are all more effective when intuition is integrated into our work and everyday life.

At the same time our world is both simple and complex, and being able to live more comfortably in the paradoxical gap that exists between the two, allows you to stop resisting it. You will find that if you are present in your life, let your emotions flow, and give yourself the gift of relaxation, your ideas will flow more easily too. You'll be more creative and insightful, and consequently your life will flow; you will not have to work as hard when you stop resisting your intuitive nature.

Intuition is a powerful energy. When you add it to the power of purpose, you will live the life you want. Do the work it takes to gather the energy you have allowed to scatter, because when you are intentionally and consciously aware, you will live a happier, more powerful life.

One night after work my daughter Joy and her friend headed west out of Montana into Idaho. They were on their way to do some shopping before Joy's wedding, and they decided to drive at night. Most likely Joy was driving too fast, but nonetheless, when they came around a bend, an enormous grizzly bear was in the road, directly in front of them in their lane. As my daughter attempted to move around the bear, the car spun in circles out of control. Then her car slid sideways, and for no earthly reason, stopped at the edge of the mountain. Shaken, the young women decided to rent a room for the night and continue their journey in the morning.

We do not always have control of everything that happens to us; however, we can use what does happen to our advantage, learn from it, and use the experience to practice making wise choices. Joy and her friend have a lot more to do in their lives, and you do too. Live your life consciously, put everything you have learned together, and use the combination to live purposefully, to live powerfully, and to live happily by your own design.

Bibliography

Abarbanel, Karin. 1994. *How to Succeed on Your Own: Overcoming the Emotional Roadblocks on the Way from Corporation to Cottage, from Employee to Entrepreneur.* New York: Henry Holt & Company.

Arredondo, Lani. 1991. *How To Present Like A Pro: Getting People to See Things Your Way.* New York: McGraw-Hill, Inc.

Bardwick, Judith M. 1991. *Danger in the Comfort Zone: From Boardroom to Mailroom – How to Break the Entitlement Habit That's Killing American Business.* New York: Amacom.

Canfield, Jack. 1993. *Chicken Soup for the Soul: 101 Stories to Open the Heart and Rekindle the Spirit.* Deerfield Beach: Health Communications.

Charan, Ram & Tichy, Noel, M. 1998. *Every Business Is a Growth Business: How Your Company Can Prosper Year After Year.* New York: Three Rivers Press.

Chiazzari, Suzy. 1998. *The Complete Book of Color: Using Color for Lifestyle, Health, and Well-Being.* Shaftesbury, Dorset: Element Books Limited.

Covey, Steven R. 1989. *The 7 Habits of Highly Effective People: Powerful Personal Lessons in Change.* New York: Simon & Schuster.

Dyer, Dr. Wayne W. 2004. *The Power of Intention: Learning to Co-create Your World Your Way.* Carlsbad: Hay Howse.

Elsea, Janet G. 1984. *The Four-Minute Sell.* New York: Simon & Schuster.

Fox, Jeffrey J. 2000. *How to Become a Rainmaker: The Rules for Getting and Keeping Customers and Clients.* New York: Hyperion.

Glassner, Barry. 1999. *The Culture of Fear: Why Americans Are Afraid of the Wrong Things.* New York: Basic Books.

Gyatso, Tenzin. His Holiness, the 14th Dalai Lama. 2000. *The Meaning of Life: Buddhist Perspectives on Cause and Effect.* Somerville: Wisdom Publications.

Hartamann, Thom. 2006. *Screwed: The Undeclared War on the Middle Class – and What We Can Do About It.* San Francisco: Berrett-Koehler Publishers.

Hawkins, David R. 2002. *Power vs Force: The Hidden Determinants of Human Behavior.* Carlsbad: Hay House. Orig. pub. 1995.

Hill, Napoleon. 1960. *Think and Grow Rich*. New York: Ballantine Books.

Keller, Jeff. 1999. *Attitude Is Everything: Change Your Attitude . . . And Change Your Life*. Tampa: INTI Publishing.

Koch, Richard. 1998. The 80/20 Principle: *The Secret to Success by Achieving More with Less*. New York: Doubleday.

Kornfield, Jack. 2000. *After the Ecstasy the Laundry: How the Heart Grows Wise on the Spiritual Path*. New York: Bantam Books.

Lavington, Camille. 1997. *You've Only Got Three Seconds: How to Make the Right Impression in Your Business and Social Life*. New York: Bantam Doubleday Dell.

Maurer, Rick. 2002. *Why Don't You Want What I want: How to Win Support for Your Ideas without Hard Sell, Manipulation, or Power Plays*. Atlanta: Bard Press.

Maysonave, Sherry. 1999. *Casual Power: How to Power Up Your Nonverbal Communication and Dress Down for Success*. Austin: Bright Books.

McGraw, Phillip C, PhD. 2001. *Self Matters: Creating Your Life from the Inside Out*. New York: Simon Schuster.

McWilliams, Peter. 1991. *Do It! Let's Get Off Our Buts*. Los Angeles: Prelude Press.

Morem, Susan. 1997. *How to Gain the Professional Edge: Achieve the Personal and Professional Image You Want*. Plymouth: Better Books.

Myss, Caroline, PhD. 1997. *Why People Don't Heal And How They Can*. New York: Three Rivers Press. Orig. Ed, Harmony Books, 2003.

Nemeth, Maria, PhD. 2000. *The Energy of Money: A Spiritual Guide to Financial and Personal Fulfillment*. New York: Ballantine. Orig. pub. 1999.

Orloff, Judith, MD. 2004. *Positive Energy: 10 Extraordinary Prescriptions for Transforming Fatigue, Stress, and Fear into Vibrance, Strength, and Love*. New York: Harmony Books.

Payne, Ruby K. 1998. *A Framework for Understanding Poverty*. Baytown: RFT Publishing.

Peters, Thomas J, Waterman, Robert H. Jr. 1982. *In Search of Excellence: Lessons from America's Best Run Companies*. New York: Harper & Row.

Phillips, Michael. 1997. *The Seven Laws of Money*. Boston: Shambhala.

Richardson, Cheryl. 1998. *Take Time for Your Life: A Coach's Seven-Step Program for Creating the Life You Want*. New York: Broadway Books.

Robey, Dan. 2003. *The Power of Positive Habits*. New York: Abritt Publishing Group.

Schultz, Mona Lisa, MD, PhD. 1998. *Awaking Intuition: Using Your Mind-Body Network for Insight and Healing*. New York: Three Rivers Press.

Seligman, Martin E, PhD. 2002. *Authentic Happiness: Using the New Positive Psychology to Realize Your Potential for Lasting Fulfillment*. New York: Simon & Schuster.

Siegel, Marc, MD. 2005. *False Alarm: The Truth About the Epidemic of Fear*. Hoboken: Jon Wiley & Sons.

Simmons, Rachel. 2003. *Odd Girl Out: The Hidden Culture of Aggression in Girls*. San Diego: Harcourt. First Harvest Edition, 2002.

Tolle, Eckhart. 2003. *Stillness Speaks*. Novato: New World Library: Publishers Group West.

Williamson, Marianne. 2002. *Everyday Grace: Having Hope, Finding Forgiveness, and Making Miracle*. New York: Riverhead Books.

Zubko, Andy. 1998. *Treasury of Spiritual Wisdom*. San Diego: Blue Dove Press. Original Edition, 1996.

Zukov, Gary. 1990. *The Seat of the Soul*. New York: Simon & Schuster.